The Manager's Concise

Guide to Risk

To Lucie,

with love and gratitude

150566

The Manager's Concise
Guide to Risk

Jihad S. Nader

JOHN WILEY & SONS LTD

British Library Cataloguing in Publication Data
A catalogue record for this book is available from the British Library

ISBN 0-471-48651-5

Project management by Originator, Gt Yarmouth (typeset in $11\frac{1}{2}/13\frac{1}{2}$pt Times)
Printed and bound in Great Britain by Antony Rowe, Chippenham, Wilts.
This book is printed on acid-free paper responsibly manufactured from sustainable forestry,
in which at least two trees are planted for each one used for paper production.

Contents

Preface

Every business firm is, in essence, a vehicle for bearing certain risks in order to generate rewards (wealth increments) for the firm's stakeholders. The management of the business enterprise in its different functional areas should therefore be viewed essentially as a process of risk management. Special emphasis should be placed on those functional areas which are concerned with managing the firm's financial resources (e.g., finance, investment, credit, treasury), as the adoption of a risk-management outlook in these areas is of critical importance to the overall management process, to the firm's profitability, and to the very survival of the firm.

To be undertaken effectively, the process of risk management must be carried out by professionals who possess the requisite expertise to perform, as fully and accurately as possible, each of the sequential tasks described below, in every business situation that calls for analysis, evaluation, and decision making. These tasks, which may be viewed as a basic flow chart of the risk-management process, are:

- Recognizing all the attendant risks and identifying them by type.
- Measuring or estimating each type of risk present.
- Estimating the return that is expected to be generated from bearing each type of risk, and comparing this expected return with an appropriate "objective" benchmark to determine if it is commensurate with the risk.
- Making a decision regarding each type of risk that is present:
  Either
  - Accept the risk if the expected return is adequate, and
  - Manage the risk by using one of the following approaches:
    - ☐ Carry the risk exposure in full and factor its price into the prices of the firm's goods and services charged to the firm's customers.
    - ☐ Reduce the risk exposure through hedging or diversification and charge the cost of hedging or diversification, plus an

adequate price for any remaining risk, to the firm's customers
through the prices of the firm's goods and services.

☐ Shift the risk exposure to another party (e.g., insurer) and
charge the insurance premium to the firm's customers
through the prices of the firm's goods and services.

Or

■ Reject the risk if, due to either or both of the following reasons,
the expected return from bearing the risk is inadequate:

■ The firm's competitive position in its market does not permit it to
increase its product and service prices to its customers by an
amount at least equivalent to the firm's costs of carrying,
reducing, or shifting the risk.

■ The market and institutional mechanisms for reducing or shifting
the risk are incomplete or do not exist; for example, the appropriate hedging and diversification instruments and types of
insurance are not available in the market, or they are only
partially available and not priced competitively.

The focus of this *Guide to Risk* is almost entirely on the first step in the
risk-management process outlined above. Written with the professional
business manager in mind, this work is intended to serve as a quick
reference that can assist the manager in recognizing and correctly identifying risk and in distinguishing between the many types and varieties of
risk that are likely to arise in the course of business and economic activity.
To a lesser extent, and using the bare minimum of mathematical or statistical development, *Guide to Risk* explains and illustrates with simple
numerical examples how some key risk concepts can be quantified and
measured.

In addition to, and perhaps more importantly than its use as a
manager's desk reference, this *Guide to Risk*—if read in its entirety—
can generate much "added value" by expanding the scope of the
manager's knowledge from those few risk concepts made familiar
through frequent encounter in a specific industry, line of business,
division of a firm, or type of transaction, to a much broader and more
comprehensive risk framework. In such a framework, the manager may
find that other, unfamiliar or seemingly irrelevant types of risk are in fact
related to or could occur concomitantly with the more familiar types, and
that those risks—previously unfamiliar or presumed irrelevant—must not
therefore be left out of the manager's analysis and decision-making
process.

I hope this *Guide to Risk* will prove useful to many in business and in the financial services community, as well as to policymakers in government and regulatory agencies concerned with setting, revising, and monitoring compliance with the rules pertaining to the various types of risk in business transactions and economic activity.

Jihad S. Nader
October 2001

Assigned Risk

The term *assigned risk* is a specialized term of automobile insurance, which defines a class of individuals to whom insurance companies either:

■ refuse to provide insurance coverage altogether; or
■ will only provide designated insurance coverage under a special *assigned risk* program.

The reason for this discriminatory treatment by insurers is usually a prior high accident record or other documented high-risk behavior by these individuals.

The existence of special *assigned risk* programs is often the result of "financial responsibility" laws or other legislation that compels insurance companies to provide such designated insurance coverage to individuals who would otherwise be treated as *uninsurable risks* by insurance companies (see *insurable risks*, p. 55). The purpose of such legislation is to ensure that accident victims, and citizens in general, are adequately insured against risks which are normally uninsurable in the market for insurance, but for which the existence of insurance coverage would be socially desirable.

Being legally compelled to cover those risks, insurance companies set the premium schedules for *assigned risk* at substantially higher levels than average, in order to receive adequate compensation.

Basis Risk

Basis risk is a term used in relation to hedging with derivative products. Particularly in the futures market, a hedge is a position taken in futures contracts, which is opposite to a position taken in the spot (cash) market. An example using interest rate futures is buying a long-term bond with the intent of holding it for a specified period, say one year, and (based on expectations of rising interest rates) simultaneously selling futures contracts on the same bond, with a close-out date of one year.

While such a hedge may be highly effective in minimizing the expected loss on liquidation of the bond position at the end of the holding period, the hedge is unlikely to perfectly eliminate the *risk of loss* (see p. 91). The reason is that there will usually be a discrepancy, throughout the holding period, between the price of the security (e.g., bond) in the spot market and its futures price (adjusted by an appropriate conversion factor). Thus, the hedger will still be concerned (right up to just before the close-out date) about *basis risk*, which is measured by the fluctuating difference between the spot price and (appropriately adjusted) futures price of the security during the holding period.

The more the basis fluctuates, the more *basis risk* there is and the more uncertain will the investor be about the net value of the position at the close-out date. However, as the close-out date approaches, the spot and futures prices of the security move closer and closer to each other, and the basis moves closer and closer to zero.

Related concepts: *foreign exchange rate risk* (p. 2); *interest rate risk* (p. 58).

Break-even Risk

Break-even risk is a component of a firm's *operating risk* (see p. 75). It arises from the possibility that:

■ a newly-established (start-up) firm might fail to reach the minimum or critical level of operations required for the firm to be economically viable; or

■ an established, ongoing firm might slide (due to a decline in demand and sales) to a level of operations below the critical level required for the firm to remain economically viable.

It is unusual for a new firm to reach its break-even level immediately after starting operations. Thus, every company is normally expected to go through a start-up phase during which the *break-even risk* is at its highest level. The main challenge facing management before and during start-up is to make this phase as short as possible.

If it becomes sufficiently clear, some time after the start of operations, that attainment of the break-even output and sales levels within a certain time frame is unforeseeable or highly unlikely, then there would be a strong case for shutting down the business, as the only rational alternative in this case would be to minimize losses.

Break-even risk can readily be assessed by analyzing the structure of operating costs in relation to revenues in the income statement.

Specifically, operating costs can be classified into two categories: fixed and variable.

Fixed Operating Costs (F)

These are the operating costs that do not change with the level of output and sales. Examples include rent, insurance, salaries of the firm's executives and administrative staff, the part of depreciation that depends on passage of time and technological obsolescence (irrespective of the rate of utilization of fixed assets), and so on.

It should be noted that interest expenses (and other costs of funds that are contractually binding on the firm and must be paid periodically, regardless of the firm's operating results) should not be included in F, because such costs are fixed financing charges; that is, they have to do with how the firm is financed, rather than with the nature of the firm's operations (industry, product, technology, market, etc.).

Variable Operating Costs (v · Q)

Where v = variable cost per unit produced and sold, and Q = number of units produced and sold). These are the operating costs that vary directly with the level of output and sales. Examples include most components of the cost of goods sold (materials, direct labor, and so on), selling, general and administrative expenses, and the part of depreciation (wear and tear and deterioration of physical assets through utilization) that depends directly on the level of business operations.

Determining the Break-even Point

Operating at the break-even point is attained when sales revenue ($p \cdot Q$; p = selling price per unit of output) is just enough to cover all the fixed and variable operating expenses of the firm. That is:

$$p \cdot Q = F + v \cdot Q$$

Therefore, the break-even quantity (the minimum quantity [in units] that must be produced and sold in order for the firm to be viable) is:

$$Q^* = F/(p - v)$$

Determining Q^* is very useful for assessing *break even risk*. The following observations are helpful in performing such an assessment:

- The larger Q^*, the higher the *break-even risk*. Stated differently, for a new company whose Q^* is large, the start-up phase—with actual $Q < Q^*$—is expected to last longer (and the attendant risk is expected to be higher) than for another company whose Q^* is small. Similarly, for an established company that has successfully passed its start-up phase (i.e., actual $Q > Q^*$), a high Q^* means that the company is exposed to greater *break-even risk* (e.g., sliding to a nonviable level of operations due to a slump in demand) than with a low Q^*.
- The break-even level of output and sales Q^* is actually a level of operations at which the firm's "contribution margin" per unit $(p - v)$ is just enough to cover the fixed operating costs (F). That is:

$$(p - v) \cdot Q^* = F$$

Accordingly, for a given F, the firm can break even at a smaller Q^* (and *break-even risk* would be lower) if management is able to increase the contribution margin per unit. This can be achieved through one or both of the following approaches:

  - pricing policy (selling at a higher p, provided competitive conditions for the firm's products, including quality and reputation, are favorable);
  - internal cost control (reducing v through more effective budgeting, cost monitoring, variance analysis, minimizing waste and operating inefficiency, and other similar internal measures).

- The higher F, the larger Q^* and the higher the *break-even risk*. In fact, the size of a firm's fixed operating costs is largely determined by the technology employed in operations. In general, advanced technologies (highly automated, non-labor-intensive) involve a higher F, while basic technologies (high rate of direct labor utilization) involve a lower F.

The preceding observation gives a perspective on the firm's choice of operating technology and the implications of that choice for the firm's *break-even risk* (and, more generally, for its *operating risk*). For example, a firm which, as part of a restructuring or re-engineering process, decides to close down some of its manufacturing operations in developed countries, and relocate to developing countries where F is lower, may in fact be reducing its *operating risk* while maintaining or increasing its operating income.

Break-even Revenue

As firms usually produce and sell many products and services, which are defined and measured in different physical units, Q^* as developed and discussed above may not be very relevant or useful for the practicalities of risk analysis. For this reason, it may be more appropriate to restate the break-even level in terms of the minimum revenue that must be generated, rather than the physical output that must be sold. This can be done in a straightforward manner, through multiplying both sides of the Q^* equation above by p and then simplifying, to obtain the break-even revenue or sales (S^*) as:

$$S^* = F/(1 - v/p)$$

One advantage of this formula is that it can readily be applied to analyze *break-even risk* by using income statement data on F and v/p, with v/p being computed as the ratio of total variable costs ($v \cdot Q$) to total sales ($p \cdot Q$), since $v \cdot Q/p \cdot Q = v/p$. This would avoid the problem of having to use a different v and a different p for each product or service produced and sold by the firm.

Finally, it should be noted that the above analysis may be applied in the assessment of *break-even risk* for a division of the firm or for any of its products separately. The latter application is particularly useful in risk evaluation for new products, as a comparison of the estimated break-even point with market prospects, for a new product may be instrumental in deciding whether to go ahead with development and launching plans for that product or to abandon these plans due to unacceptable *break-even risk*.

Business Risk

For any business enterprise, the term *business risk* may generally be viewed as synonymous with *operating risk* (see p. 75). This is the risk (possible fluctuations in net income) that arises from the nature and characteristics of the products or services produced and sold by the firm.

Importantly, *business (operating) risk* does not include the effects of the financing mix (debt vs. equity) on the variability of the firm's net income; such effects are defined and analyzed separately as *financing risk* effects (see p. 36).

In the case of commercial banks and similar depository institutions, *business risk* is broader than *operating risk*. In fact, *operating risk* is just one of the components of a bank's *business risk*.

The *business risk* of commercial banks deserves special consideration, in view of the different nature of the products and services produced by banks, and those produced by nonfinancial institutions. A bank's products consist mainly of loans and investments. As such, a bank's *business risk* consists of a number of main components, namely:

■ credit (default) risk (p. 13);
■ investment risk (p. 63);
■ operating risk (p. 75);
■ liquidity risk (p. 66);
■ fiduciary (fidelity) risk (p. 35);
■ fraud risk (p. 39).

Call Risk

Call risk (also known as *prepayment risk*) arises in connection with bank loans or with investments in marketable debt instruments. This risk affects the lender or holder of the debt instrument whenever the borrower or issuer of the debt instrument has the right to prepay the loan or call the debt issue before its maturity.

From the borrower's perspective, such prepayment or early call is favorable—and therefore becomes more probable—if market interest rates have fallen to a level sufficiently below the interest rate on the loan or the yield to maturity on the debt instrument (e.g., bond) to generate net savings from loan refinancing or bond refunding at the lower market rate of interest. In this case the net savings to the borrower or bond issuer, from refinancing or refunding, would be larger—and hence prepayment or early call would be more attractive:

■ the longer is the remaining loan term or term to maturity of the bond;
■ the lower is the prepayment penalty or early call premium payable by the borrower or bond issuer; and
■ the lower are the transaction costs (commissions, legal fees, issue costs, etc.) associated with loan refinancing or bond refunding.

The reason *call risk* is of concern to the lender or holder of the debt instrument is that the event of prepayment or call deprives the lender or investor in long-term debt securities from the rate of return initially expected at the outset of the loan or investment, since the market interest rate for the remaining term is now below the initially expected rate. In other words, prepayment or early call is a potential source of *reinvestment risk* (see p. 88) to the lender or bondholder. For this reason, lenders (e.g., banks) usually include a *prepayment penalty* clause as a standard feature in long-term loan contracts, with the stipulated penalty diminishing over the term of the loan. Similarly, investors in bonds normally expect to find a *call premium schedule* stipulated in the indentures of long-term bonds which have a *call feature*.

For such callable bonds, the *call premium* payable by the issuer is highest at the earliest permissible call date, and typically diminishes steadily thereafter. If no early *call premium* is stipulated, callable bonds would sell at a discount below the market value of similar "straight" (noncallable) bonds, as investors would otherwise buy the straight bonds and completely avoid bearing the *call risk*.

Cash Flow Risk (see *Investment Risk*, p. 63)

Catastrophic Risk

Catastrophic risk affects industries and firms whose financial assets are exposed to catastrophic natural perils, such as earthquakes, hurricanes, volcanic eruptions, and so on. Primarily, it is a type of risk that concerns the insurance and reinsurance industry. The history of this industry offers many examples of catastrophic events that resulted in huge losses for insurers and reinsurers. Examples include Hurricane Betsy in 1965, Hurricane Andrew in 1992, the Northridge Earthquake in 1994, and the Kobe Earthquake in 1995.

Although catastrophic risk is usually considered as an outcome of natural perils, one nonnatural peril, terrorism, has emerged in recent years as a source of risk whose consequences for the insurance and reinsurance industry appear increasingly capable of attaining the same dimensions as those of catastrophic risk. The September 11, 2001 attacks on the World Trade Center and the Pentagon are the most notorious example, with claims estimated to reach as much as $70 billion.

Catastrophic Risk Management

The traditional approach to catastrophic risk management is to spread such risks through the insurance and reinsurance system. However, the effectiveness of this approach may be diminishing due to the fact that catastrophic events may threaten the capital adequacy or wipe out the capital of a number of insurance firms at the same time. This highlights the insurance and reinsurance industry's potential exposure to systemic risk or contagion risk as a result of catastrophic risk.

An alternative approach to managing catastrophic risk, which is receiving much attention, is the creation of specially designed instruments ("cat" securities) for sharing catastrophic risks through the capital markets.

It should also be noted that major advances have been made in recent years in the quantitative assessment and modeling of catastrophic risk. The main advantages of these developments are the improved ability of insurers to set adequate prices for the catastrophic risks they underwrite, and the improved ability to diversify and manage these risks through the use of portfolio approaches.

Collection Risk

Collection risk is a type of *credit risk* (see p. 13) which arises from merchants' (or other payees') acceptance of check payments by their customers (or other payors). It is the risk that at the end of the check-clearing process the customer's check may be returned unpaid because the funds available in the customer's checking account are insufficient.

Initially, *collection risk* is borne by the merchant, who is essentially in the same position as a lender to the customer. Furthermore, the "loan" to the customer is an interest-free loan, which enables the customer to enjoy the early possession and use of the purchased goods during the period that the check remains in the check-clearing process. In other words, a check payment provides the customer with a float, while the merchant incurs the opportunity cost (equal to the float) of the forgone interest on the amount paid by check.

Clearly, the longer the check-clearing process is, the more advantageous is the float to the customer. For this reason, many companies in North America which make frequent payments by check have adopted a remote dispersal and lockbox system as a standard part of their cash management, whose purpose is to cause their checks to follow a long and circuitous collection route in order to maximize their float from check payments. To counter this practice, merchants typically offer discounts on cash payments, thereby reducing or eliminating the check float and making it less favorable, or simply unfavorable, for their customers to pay by check.

The main question that must be addressed with check payments is: Who bears the *collection risk*? The answer to this question is to be sought in the design and the legal and regulatory framework of the check-clearing system. Depending on this framework, which varies from one country to another, the *collection risk* arising from a check payment may be borne by any one or a combination of the following parties:

- the merchant (payee) who accepts a check payment;
- the merchant's bank;
- the customer's (payor's) bank.

Collection risk to the payor's or payee's bank can be entirely eliminated through the use of direct funds transfers from payor to payee, instead of check payments. The best example of this practice may be found in European banking, where the use of Giro accounts is widespread.

Under the Giro system, the payor instructs his bank to transfer funds from his Giro account, to the payee's account with another bank. If the payor does not have sufficient funds in his Giro account, the payment will not be made and the transaction in whose consideration the payment was to be made would not take place. In this way, any *credit risk* arising from the transaction is borne entirely by the payee, and is greatly reduced by the speed of the Giro system and the definitive information it provides regarding the funds' transfer.

Competitive Risk

Competitive risk is a type of *exchange rate risk* (see p. 32) which affects multinational firms through their foreign subsidiaries. It arises from the possible effects of fluctuations in the currency of a country in which:

■ a subsidiary of a multinational firm carries out direct production operations (e.g., manufacturing, assembly) in a foreign country (the host country);

■ these operations utilize raw materials, labor, and other direct-cost components from the host country (i.e., their cost is paid in the currency of the host country); and

■ the product of the subsidiary is sold in foreign countries other than the host country (i.e., the subsidiary's revenue from those sales is received in the host country's currency).

In this case, appreciation in the currency of the host country would make the product of the subsidiary less competitive in the foreign markets where it is sold, resulting in lower sales and profits to the subsidiary and its parent. In the opposite event, depreciation in the currency of the host country would increase the competitiveness of the subsidiary's product and result in increased sales and profits to the subsidiary and its parent.

It is interesting to note that currency depreciation in a given country is believed to be an attractive development that favors foreign direct-investment flows into that country (e.g., through setting up foreign subsidiaries of multinationals), while currency appreciation is considered unfavorable to such flows. In the present context, this observation may be interpreted to mean that host countries whose currencies are expected to undergo sustained long-term depreciation offer multinationals an opportunity to generate higher profits from the *competitive risk* component of *exchange rate risk*.

Another related observation is that undertaking foreign direct investment in numerous host countries whose economies are unrelated or dissimilar may generate a "portfolio effect" (see *portfolio risk*, p. 86) through diversifying the *competitive risk* borne by a multinational firm.

Confiscation Risk

Confiscation risk is one of the components which make up the *political risk* exposure (see p. 84) of a firm that has investments in foreign lands. This type of risk arises whenever there is a nonnegligible probability that a foreign government might take over ("nationalize") the firm's investments (e.g., land, plant and equipment, etc.) without offering any compensation (cf. *expropriation risk*, p. 34).

Contagion Risk

Contagion risk arises as a possible consequence of the failure of a depository financial institution such as a commercial bank. For example, the collapse of a major bank might cause an abrupt erosion of confidence in the banking system as a whole, resulting in a run on the banking industry due to mass panic among depositors.

This rapid sequence of events might lead to sudden and serious strains on the liquidity of other banks. As a result, some banks which are otherwise safe, sound, and solvent might themselves collapse if the strain on their liquidity is sustained, unless there is timely and effective intervention by the Central Bank (on an emergency basis) to provide these banks with enough liquidity to ride out the panic run.

Various risk factors might contribute to *contagion risk*, including *payment system risk* (see p. 80), inadequate diversification of *country risk* (see below) within the banking system, and *interbank risk* (see p. 57).

Assessment and control of *contagion risk* is an important area of bank supervision and regulation. For such purposes, some measure of the sensitivity of each commercial bank to the failure of other banks may be used.

Country Risk

Country risk is a term that encompasses a wide range of risks involved in making international lending decisions and the management of international loans. Such risks are additional to and distinct from the risks that normally arise in domestic lending. They are usually classified into two broad categories: *sovereign risk* (see p. 98) and *transfer risk* (see p. 116).

Those risks which make up *country risk* stem from various political, economic, or social factors that may affect (positively or negatively) the expected profitability of loans or equity investments made in a given foreign country. On the downside, not only the profitability but even the recovery of such loans or investments may be put in question due to *country risk* factors.

It is important to note that the definition and assessment of *country risk* should include not only the ability but also the willingness of borrowers (especially sovereign borrowers) in a foreign country to discharge their obligations under a loan or equity investment made in that country.

Financial institutions regularly assess and monitor their overall *country risk* exposure in the various foreign countries where they have outstanding loans and other risk assets. Some indicators used in this regard may be based on the simple, judgmental assessment of social, economic, and political developments in each foreign country. Other indicators may consist of more clearly defined, quantitative macro-economic measures. The following list summarizes the most important indicators used in gauging *country risk*:

- the foreign government's policies regarding liberalization vs. restriction of economic and business life, international trade flows, and the allocation of resources, as indicated by tariffs and other trade barriers, price and interest rate controls, exchange rate "fixing" through legislation, regulation, or government intervention in the foreign exchange markets, restrictions on foreign direct investment, on bank branching, on remittance of funds, and so on;
- the foreign government's predisposition to use debt for financing public expenditures in response to social pressures and demands for a higher standard of living;
- the rate of return on government expenditures funded with foreign debt, relative to the cost of that debt;
- the rate at which the money supply (and inflation) in the foreign country has been increasing;
- the volatility in the foreign country's terms of trade as indicated by concentration of its exports in a small number of primary products vs. diversification of its production and export base over a large number of products;
- the ratio of the foreign country's government deficit to gross national product (GNP);
- the foreign country's debt service ratio (i.e., the total foreign exchange earnings from exports, divided by foreign exchange earnings used for interest and principal repayment on debts outstanding to other countries);
- the ratio of current account deficit to export earnings;
- the ratio of net interest payments on the country's foreign debt to its foreign (hard) currency reserves.

Related concept: *political risk* (p. 84)

Coupon Reinvestment Risk

Coupon reinvestment risk is one of the two components of *interest rate risk* (see p. 58) which affect bonds and bond portfolios. The other component is *price risk* (see p. 86). These two components always have opposite effects on *interest rate risk*. Specifically, when there is a rise in market interest rates, a bond's market price falls, but the investor can reinvest the fixed coupon income at the higher market rates of interest during the remaining term of the bond. When there is a fall in market interest rates, bond prices increase, but the fixed coupon income can only be reinvested at the lower market rates.

Because of their opposite effects, the *coupon reinvestment risk* component and the *price risk* component can be offset against each other, resulting in a perfect hedge against *interest rate risk*. For an illustration of such an "immunization" strategy, which uses duration, see the section on *interest rate risk* (p. 58).

Credit Risk

Credit risk, also known as *default risk*, is by far the most significant risk borne by a commercial bank. It also arises from transactions undertaken by a business firm whenever the firm agrees to deliver goods or services to customers on a noncash basis (i.e., on credit). Likewise, investments in bonds, notes, bills, and other debt instruments give rise to *credit risk* for which the compensation required by the investor is factored into the interest rate (yield or discount rate) on the instrument.

The source of *credit risk* is the possibility that the borrower may become unable or unwilling to fulfill his contractual obligations to the lender, through the full and timely payment of interest and repayment of the loan principal.

Credit risk carries special significance and is a serious threat to the banking institution because of the relatively small proportion of bank equity financing in comparison with the capital proportion of ordinary (nonbank) business firms. Indeed, if the *credit risk* borne by a bank is excessive, it may bring about the bankruptcy of the bank itself due to the effect of bad loan "write-offs" on the bank's net worth.

The seriousness of *credit risk* for a bank can be illustrated with a simple example. Consider a bank which has a loan portfolio of $1,000

consisting of ten loans of $100 each, with a maturity of one year. If the
annual interest rate on each loan is 10%, then the total interest revenue
on the loan portfolio is 10% × $1,000 = $100 at the end of the year. Now
consider what would happen to the loan portfolio if one of the ten
borrowers defaults and becomes permanently unable to repay the loan
(e.g., due to bankruptcy). The loan principal (asset) of $100 must be
written off as a loss, resulting in a complete wipe-out of the expected
revenue of $100 on the initial loan portfolio.

This means that because of the loss taken on just one loan the
remaining nine loans, with a principal of $900, will in effect have been
made as interest-free loans, while the bank must continue to honor its
contractual interest obligations to its depositors.

The preceding example is an over-simplification intended for illustration only. In actual fact, the treatment of problem loans (and the actual
outcome of *credit risk*) in a bank follows a well-structured accounting and
control process which allows a clear differentiation between varying levels
of *credit risk*. This process may be outlined as follows:

- A bank sets aside a portion of its periodic profits (in the income
  statement) and its equity (in the balance sheet) to cover possible
  "bad debt" losses in the event that some borrowers may default.
- The portion of periodic profits set aside for this purpose appears in
  the income statement as a "provision for bad debt losses." In most tax
  regimes, this provision is tax deductible.
- The portion of equity (net worth) set aside for covering possible bad
  debt losses is disclosed in the balance sheet as a "reserve for bad debt
  losses." It is treated as a contra-asset which appears underneath, and
  is deducted from the total loans outstanding in the bank's balance
  sheet.
- The accounting treatment for setting aside this coverage is: debit
  "provision for bad debt losses" and credit "reserve for bad debt
  losses."
- The preceding treatment is normally performed for loans, as necessary,
  at the time of their approval by management. The amount thus set
  aside depends on management's assessment of the *credit risk* involved
  in each loan. This assessment takes into account the overall credit-
  worthiness of each borrowing customer, as portrayed by the customer's financial statements, cash flow forecasts, present and future
  market share, management quality and expertise, product and market
  diversification, and other key factors used in *credit risk* assessment. Of
  course, the amount set aside (in the manner described above) increases

with the assessed *credit risk* of each loan applicant. Furthermore, the bank's management may increase the amount of the "provision for bad debt losses" and the "reserve for bad debt losses" for any given loan if, at any point in time during its term, the *credit risk* of that loan is believed to have increased.

- As soon as a borrower fails to make a scheduled payment on an outstanding loan, that payment is treated as past due and the bank begins to accrue past due interest, on the assumption that the missed payment will eventually be received.

- The past due interest is debited as an addition to the outstanding loan principal in the balance sheet, and credited as interest revenue in the income statement.

- If the loan is still past due after a certain period set by regulation (e.g., 90 days in the USA), it must be included in a special report on past due loans which the bank is required to submit periodically to the regulatory authorities (the Central Bank). Meanwhile, the bank will continue to accrue interest revenue on the past due loan.

- If the loan remains past due, at some point the bank must stop accruing interest revenue on the loan. In other words, the loan will no longer be considered an earning asset of the bank. The point in time at which a past due loan is placed on nonaccrual status is left largely to the judgment of the bank's management regarding the current and future ability of the borrower to resume the interest payments on the loan. The more conservative is the bank's management, the sooner will a past due loan be placed on nonaccrual status and the more representative will be the bank's financial statement disclosure of its true loan portfolio quality.

- Eventually, if the loan is still carried on a nonaccrual basis, it must be placed in default. Bank supervisors and regulators play an important role in bringing about this transition in loan status without undue delay. Without bank supervision and regulation, some bank managements may be over-optimistic and may misjudge the prospects for the return of a past due loan from nonaccrual status to current (active) status.

- When a loan is placed in default, the bank deducts the entire outstanding balance from the "reserve for bad debt losses" in the balance sheet; that is, the bank debits the contra-asset "reserve for bad debt losses" and credits the asset "loans" by the amount of the loan in default. In this way, maintaining an adequate "reserve for bad debt losses acts to shield the bank's net worth against *actual* losses resulting from the write-off of bad loans.

■ Instead of being recognized at the time of their actual occurrence, losses from bad loans are accounted for as *potential* losses, at the outset of each loan, when the bank's revenue is reduced by the "provision for bad debt losses" set aside (in the income statement) in consideration of each loan approved by the bank. This is an appropriate conservative approach in that the bank reduces its periodic income available for its owners by estimated future loan losses before the fact, rather than reducing the owners' equity (net worth) by actual loan losses after the fact.

■ If part or all of a loan previously placed in default is eventually recovered by the bank, the amount recovered is deducted from the total outstanding balance of loans in default. The result is that only the net balance of bad loans, after recoveries, is actually written off by deducting it from the "reserve for bad debt losses" in the balance sheet (as described above).

Currency Risk (see *Exchange Rate Risk,* p. 32)

Currency Inconvertibility Risk

Currency inconvertibility risk is one of the components of *political risk* (see p. 84) which affects international investments. It is the risk of an unanticipated change in the political environment of a foreign country, leading either to direct action by that country's government constraining or prohibiting conversion of the country's local currency to hard currencies, or to the total absence of demand for that currency in the international foreign exchange markets. In either case, investors from other countries would effectively be put in the same situation that would arise from restrictions on repatriation of invested capital or investment earnings (see *repatriation risk*, p. 88).

In the USA, Canada, and several other industrialized nations, firms can purchase special insurance against possible losses from *currency inconvertibility risk* and other components of *political risk*. Such insurance is offered by specialized government agencies (e.g., the Overseas Private Investment Corporation in the USA and the Export Development Corporation in Canada).

Daylight Overdraft Risk (see *Payment System Risk*, p. 80)

Default Risk (see *Credit Risk*, p. 13)

Deflation Risk

Deflation risk has emerged as one of the most topical and widely debated economic issues in the late 1990s. It is also an issue which continues to stir up controversy as to: (1) what deflation is and whether it is now present in various economies (especially the developed ones); and (2) whether deflation, if present (especially in the developing industrial economies), is really the source of any risk at all to the developed economies.

To gain an understanding of this issue, it is necessary to present the main observations and views of each side in the controversy. But first, it is prudent to present simple definitions of deflation and related terms.

The Terminology of Price-level Changes: Hyperinflation, Inflation, Disinflation, and Deflation

In the mid-1990s, many economists and financial market analysts in the world's leading industrial nations (especially in the USA) were leaning towards the view that the sustained downward trend in the price level had already breached the lower boundary of the "normal" inflation–disinflation range, and that a more extreme and potentially threatening state of affairs called "deflation" had already set in.

The opposite state of affairs, the upward trend, is known as "hyper-inflation." Hyperinflation is a familiar term which describes rampant price-level increases, and it is often used in discussions of the economic mismanagement and political uncertainty that resulted in three-digit and four-digit inflation rates in the economies of numerous developing countries in the 1970s and 1980s.

Deflation must be distinguished from disinflation, its more "normal" cousin. Disinflation describes the outcome of the process through which the inflation rate is brought down whenever further increases in this rate are believed to be damaging to the efficiency of the price system, which is the cornerstone of any market economy. In the industrialized economies, this process is usually cyclical, and it is helped along through the use of monetary policy (e.g., "tight" money) and other macroeconomic policy tools. Thus, there are two important properties which make disinflation different from deflation. First, disinflation is usually the result of a *managed* process. Second, the outcome of this process is a reduced but still *positive* inflation rate.

Deflation, on the other hand, is defined as a pervasive and sustained decline in the general price level to a point where the inflation rate is *negative*, bringing about a generalized decline in *real* values in the economy. In a deflationary environment, real prices fall steadily in the product markets (e.g., falling real prices of consumer and industrial goods and services) and in the factor markets (e.g., declining real wages, land prices, rates of return on invested capital, and so on), and there are growing fears of a *depression*. Depressions occur whenever falling real prices cause the actual real gross domestic product (GDP) to drop far below the potential real GDP. A mild decline in real GDP is called a *recession*, and is not considered worrisome, as it occurs during normal cyclical downturns in economic activity.

The Deflation-risk Scenario in the Late 1990s

Proponents of the view that a serious risk of worldwide deflation is looming have based their argument on a diverse assortment of observations and economic indicators, the most important of which are summarized below:

- credit-restrictive policies in the G-7 countries, where monetary policy continues to be driven by fears of inflation;
- continued fiscal restraint and contraction in government spending in the G-7 countries, aimed at attaining balanced budgets through slashing deficits;
- sharp declines in real wages in the USA, as a result of ongoing defense budget cuts and corporate restructuring, which have eliminated a large number of highly-paid jobs;
- falling real prices of residential property, and weakening office rentals and land prices in major urban centers in many developed countries;
- huge drops in the Japanese stock market since the late 1980s, and the sustained downward trend in wholesale prices in Japan;

■ the long-standing overvaluation of the Deutschemark, which has greatly hurt German exports and has contributed to halting real growth in the German economy;

■ the presence of a worldwide "glut" in the product markets due largely to the supply of competitive products from Southeast Asia and other developing countries, and the existence of huge excess productive capacity, especially in the developed countries;

■ currency collapses in a number of industrially significant developing countries such as Mexico and, more recently, the countries of Southeast Asia, and the resulting huge declines in real wages in these countries;

■ the belief that the collapse of the Southeast Asian currencies will further aggravate the product market glut for the developed countries by inundating their markets with price-competitive imports and wiping out the ability of firms in the developed countries to set prices at profitable levels.

The Opposite (Mainstream) View

In the face of the preceding observations, central bankers, government policymakers, and most mainstream economists continue to hold firmly to the view that the risk of true deflation (as opposed to disinflation), and of any ensuing depression, has long been eradicated from the economic scene of the developed nations through the effective implementation of government stabilization policies. Furthermore, they discredit the deflation-risk theory as being an assemblage of unfounded interpretations of various indicators, which actually point to a normal process of disinflationary adjustment and not to looming deflation or to a global depression in the making.

In particular, adherents to the mainstream view discredit the notion that the crisis in Southeast Asia (especially the product "glut" described above) is now beginning to spill over to the developed nations, and that this is a deflationary development whose magnitude will inevitably sink those nations into economic depression. In response to this scenario, mainstream opponents refer to the fact that the entire Southeast Asia region is too small a trading partner with the USA and the other leading industrial nations to pose any serious risks from such spillover effects.

The Deflation-risk Theory: Winners and Losers

In the event that the deflation scenario should unfold, an analysis of the effects of this scenario would suggest the following main winners and losers:

Winners

- Consumers, because of the downward pressure on prices of the global product "glut" and the intensifying price competition in the product markets.
- Buyers of industrial goods, because excess productive capacity would lower demand for these goods and reduce their prices.
- Investors in long-term fixed-income securities, especially long-term Treasury bonds, which do not pay coupon interest (i.e., zero-coupon or pure discount bonds), because deflation (and falling market interest rates) would have favorable effects on the market prices of these instruments without the negative coupon reinvestment effects.

Losers

- Producers and sellers (firms), because of the downward pressure on prices, shrinking net profits, or profits turning into losses.
- Investors in common stocks of firms whose product prices, sales and profits are highly exposed to the downward pressures of deflation (e.g., stocks of manufacturing firms which face intensifying price competition from developing countries, but not stocks of services firms for which such competition is insignificant or non-existent).

Deposit Cost Risk

Deposit cost risk is the uncertainty attaching to the price (interest rate) that a bank must pay for the deposits it uses to fund either a specific loan or its entire loan portfolio. *Deposit cost risk* arises from possible fluctuations in the market interest rate on deposits, and as such, it is a component of *interest rate risk* (see p. 58) for banks and other depository financial institutions.

Specifically, *deposit cost risk* applies to bank deposits whose maturity is shorter than the maturity of the (fixed-rate) loans funded with these deposits. At maturity of the deposits, the loans would still be outstanding and must continue to be funded until their final repayment date. In the event of a rise in market interest rates, new deposits would cost the bank more than the deposits which had just matured, while the contractually-fixed interest rate on the still outstanding loan would remain unchanged. This would squeeze the net interest spread on the loan for the remainder of its term, and may even make the spread negative. The opposite would occur in the event of a fall in market interest rates, and the bank's net interest spread (profit) on its fixed-rate loans would become larger.

The management of *deposit cost risk* is part of overall *interest rate risk* management, and various techniques of asset-liability management may be used in this process. One such technique is perfect matching (zero maturity gap or zero duration gap) of the deposits to the loans they are used to fund. Another simple and widely used method for reducing *deposit rate risk* is to apply a compensating balance requirement as a condition for granting loans.

Compensating balances are non-interest earning deposits maintained at the bank by borrowing clients. They involve minimal administrative costs and no promotional costs to the bank. These substantial, virtually costless, sources of funds are also much more stable than ordinary deposits which are held at the bank by non-borrowing clients as they (compensating balances) are unlikely to be suddenly withdrawn as long as the loans to the clients who own them are still outstanding. Thus, compensating balances can be used as an inexpensive source of funds for making new loans, while minimizing *deposit rate risk*.

Diversifiable Risk (see *Unsystematic Risk*, p. 119)

Downside Risk

A prior reading of the discussion of *total risk* (p. 111) is a prerequisite for understanding the following discussion of *downside risk*.

Several alternative but closely related definitions of *downside risk* have been developed conceptually, which are mostly based on observed investor behavior or on applications and practices in corporate finance and in the financial services industry. The most notable of these definitions are:

- *downside risk* as the maximum possible loss from a prospect whose outcome is uncertain (asset, security, investment, or project);
- *downside risk* as the probability of loss from an uncertain prospect;
- *downside risk* as possible deviations below a target level of wealth or a target rate of return.

As indicated by these definitions, *downside risk* is concerned with the pessimistic side of investment behavior through its total emphasis on the investors' or decision makers' aversion to loss or to shortfalls from targets. This emphasis may be well placed in situations where a highly conservative approach to investment is required, or where institutional decision makers are bound by a fiduciary responsibility (see *fiduciary risk*, p. 35) which imposes standards of prudence on their investment decisions.
    The measurement of *downside risk* involves:

- defining all possible outcomes (wealth levels or rates of return) below an expected or target outcome;
- assigning probabilities to these downside outcomes;
- computing a probability-weighted average of the squared deviations of downside outcomes from the expected value and using this average (called the semi-variance) as a measure of *downside risk*.

To illustrate *downside risk*, consider the possible market prices of two stocks, *A* and *B* with their corresponding probabilities:

A	*Prob(A)*	*B*	*Prob(B)*
$1	0.3	$1	0.1
$2	0.4	$2	0.1
$3	0.2	$3	0.3
$4	0.1	$4	0.5
	1.0		1.0

The means, variances (measures of *total risk*), and semi-variances (measures of *downside risk*) of the prices of these two stocks are:

■ Means

$$E(A) = (\$1 \times 0.3) + (\$2 \times 0.4) + (\$3 \times 0.2) + (\$4 \times 0.1) = \$2.1$$

$$E(B) = (\$1 \times 0.1) + (\$2 \times 0.1) + (\$3 \times 0.3) + (\$4 \times 0.5) = \$3.2$$

■ Variances

$$\mathrm{Var}(A) = [(\$1 - \$2.1)^2 \times (0.3)] + [(\$2 - \$2.1)^2 \times (0.4)]$$
$$+ [(\$3 - \$2.1)^2 \times (0.2)] + [(\$4 - \$2.1)^2 \times (0.1)]$$
$$= 0.89 \ \$^2$$

$$\mathrm{Var}(B) = [(\$1 - \$3.2)^2 \times (0.1)] + [(\$2 - \$3.2)^2 \times (0.1)]$$
$$+ [(\$3 - \$3.2)^2 \times (0.3)] + [(\$4 - \$3.2)^2 \times (0.5)]$$
$$= 0.96 \ \$^2$$

■ Semi-variances (SV)

$$\mathrm{SV}(A) = [(\$1 - \$2.1)^2 \times (0.3)] + [(\$2 - \$2.1)^2 \times (0.4)]$$
$$= 0.367 \ \$^2$$

$$\mathrm{SV}(B) = [(\$1 - \$3.2)^2 \times (0.1)] + [(\$2 - \$3.2)^2 \times (0.1)]$$
$$+ [(\$3 - \$3.2)^2 \times (0.3)]$$
$$= 0.640 \ \$^2$$

A comparison of these two stocks' *total risk* and *downside risk* shows that Stock *B* has slightly more *total risk* than Stock *A* (0.96 vs. 0.89), but it has substantially more *downside risk* than Stock *A* (0.640 vs. 0.367).

In the stock market, a simple strategy for minimizing *downside risk* involves selecting stocks which have moderate price/earning (*P/E*) multiples in comparison with their industry norms, while avoiding "high-flying" stocks which are trading at *P/E* multiples much higher than their industry norms. This strategy is especially effective if the stock also has an above average dividend yield which supports the stock price against a nose dive in the event of a market downturn.

Dynamic Risk

The term *dynamic risk* is used in reference to the risk of loss arising from economy-wide fluctuations, corrections and adjustments. Examples of these fluctuations, which may cause many individuals and business firms to incur direct or indirect losses, include: advances in technology (resulting in obsolescence of the existing technology); changes in output, income and the price level, shifts in consumers' attitudes, tastes and preferences, downsizing, layoffs, and so on. The term is particularly useful for distinguishing *dynamic risks* from other risks (see *static risk*, p. 101) which are generally independent of economy-wide changes.

While the immediate short-term effects of such *dynamic risks* are usually adverse for many, their long-term effects are normally expected to be beneficial for society as a whole since those risks arise from periodic corrections and adjustments of an inefficient resource allocation within the economy to a more efficient one.

E-banking Risks

Since the advent of the Internet starting in the early 1990s, banks around the globe have been quick to recognize that their continued competitiveness, profitability, and their very survival will depend increasingly on their ability to innovate and adapt their products, services, processes, and delivery mechanisms to the rapidly expanding, technologically complex new environment of e-banking. For the most part, this ongoing transition has involved the introduction of online financial services which, in essence, supplement (rather than replace) the banks' "traditional" products and services and provide around-the-clock access to these services from virtually anywhere in the world.

The rapid transition to the e-banking environment has presented bankers with seemingly new types of risk that call for the development of new tools for detection, prevention, and control as part of an expanded risk management framework. In fact, many of these "new" types of risk are only new manifestations of familiar "old" risks present in the traditional banking environment. What is really new is that the e-banking environment has made it possible for "old" risks to present themselves in previously unknown and much more complex ways and with potentially higher frequency and severity than in the traditional banking environment. In general, the greater the monetary value of an e-banking transaction, and the larger the number of parties to and individuals involved in processing the transaction, the higher is the bank's exposure to e-banking risks.

Examples of these e-banking risks are provided below.

New Manifestations of Traditional Banking Risks

Security Risk (External Breach)–Examples

- Hackers use the Internet to enter and corrupt bank systems.
- Unauthorized parties use the Internet to gain access to banks' confidential customer information or to intercept, disrupt, or divert e-banking transactions in process.
- Viruses are successfully "deposited" into banks' computer and tele-communications systems via the Internet, destroying data, disrupting operations, and wreaking havoc.

Fraud Risk (External)–Examples

- Hackers or fraudsters use intercepted or stolen credit card data to perform Internet shopping transactions.
- The anonymous environment of the Internet makes it easier for high-risk credit applicants to defraud banks by submitting online credit applications containing false financial and personal information. Many bankers and risk managers believe that credit application fraud poses the biggest risk in the e-banking environment.

Fraud Risk (Internal)–Example

- Bank employees who have access to account data and bank records use this information to make Internet withdrawals of funds from bank customers' accounts.

Illegal Activity Risk–Example

- The anonymous, paperless environment of the Internet may make the work of money launderers (drug and contraband dealers, organized crime organizations, etc.) much easier and faster, and much more difficult for banks to detect.

Repudiation Risk–Examples

■ An e-banking transaction (funds transfer, payment to a third party, etc.) is initiated by a bank customer from a remote computer or other device (e.g., mobile telephone using WAP or other m-banking technology) and is properly carried out by the bank. The customer then denies having authorized the transaction and requests reimbursement.

■ In the broader framework of e-commerce, and especially in e-banking transactions carried out under letters of credit and other documentary credit instruments provided through online application, an e-bank may have to deal with various other situations involving repudiation. For example, if either counter-party (importer or exporter) denies that an order for goods was ever made or received, or denies that there was an application made to the bank to issue a letter of credit in connection with a business-to-business import–export transaction, then the repudiation risk to either or both of the counter-parties may translate into repudiation risk for the bank.

Information/Telecommunication Technology Infrastructure Risk–Example

■ Internal bank systems, intranets and/or the Internet (www), or other external network may slow down, become unreliable for the secure and timely completion of transactions, or may completely break down or come to a halt, resulting in losses to banks and their customers and in possible legal liability and reputational risk for the banks.

■ The much feared Year 2000 (Y2K) Problem (see p. 50), which in the late 1990s became a major preoccupation of financial institutions, regulatory authorities, business firms, computer hardware and software developers, and individual end users worldwide, is perhaps the most extreme and pervasive example to date of the potential problems that might arise from information/telecommunication technology infrastructure risk.

Sources

■ The key factors underlying this type of risk include inadequate investment in technology infrastructure, security, maintenance, and up-grading.

■ Another potential source of this risk is the ability of external parties (e.g., competitors, environmental or other special interest groups, unions, etc.) to wage volume attacks that jam traffic on a designated firm's website and delay or prevent customers from accessing that site, causing significant loss of business and potential legal liability to the firm. It should be interesting to note that it may be useful and highly representative to coin terms like "e-picketing" or "e-demonstration" for describing the Internet-age equivalents of two familiar and commonly used forms of protest in the industrial age.

Reputational Risk—Examples

■ Many of the preceding e-banking risks may generate reputational risk for the bank. Security breaches, fraud, technology-related slowdowns in e-banking service and, in general, any Internet-related cause of loss to a bank's customers may damage the bank's reputation, tarnish its image and be detrimental to its profitability and competitiveness.

■ Equally damaging to a bank's reputation is the detection, by the bank itself or by regulatory or law enforcement bodies, of illegal activity (e.g., money laundering) being successfully carried out through its e-banking services, even though the bank customers usually do not sustain losses as a result of such activity.

■ Another source of reputational risk to an e-bank or e-business firm is third-party reputational and ethical risk. For example, the bank's web page may contain links to the sites of other firms that may be essential parties to certain transactions; for example, selected insurance company links for completing mortgage loan applications, car dealership links for car loan applications, etc. Alternatively, such links may be included in the e-bank's web page as a paid promotional service. In using these links, the bank's customers may project any negative experiences (slow service, unethical practices, losses, etc.) with these third parties on the reputation of the e-bank itself. Legal liability to the bank in such cases should not be ruled out.

Legal/Regulatory Risk—Examples

■ A financial institution may find itself in noncompliance with new laws, rules, regulations or statutory standards and criteria governing e-business. For example, concerning web page design, layout, disclosure quality, and informational content; security and consumer protection requirements, tax treatment of online transactions, etc. Such noncompliance may result in penalties or legal liability for the bank, and ensuring compliance at all times will normally require the bank to incur additional costs such as monitoring, audit, and other professional fees paid to experts and legal consultants.

■ Changes in different countries' legal and regulatory environments may make certain e-banking services inaccessible or illegal in those countries.

Tools for the Management and Control of E-Banking Risks

Rapid advances in information technology are continually producing applications and solutions that provide banks, corporations, and other organizations involved in e-business with a wide range of tools for the prevention, detection, control, and ongoing management of risks encountered in the Internet environment. Examples of the most widely used tools are provided below.

Security/Fraud Risk

Tools include:

■ firewalls;
■ passwords;
■ smart cards;
■ encryption;
■ ongoing anti-virus scanning of computer and telecommunication systems and networks;
■ ongoing testing and surveillance of systems and networks for possible security breaches.

Credit Application Fraud Risk

Tools include:

■ use of credit bureau information and external databases on fraud attempts;
■ front-end screening of online credit applicants.

Drawback
It must be recognized that the use of such tools is likely to result in a slowdown of customer service. The e-bank must therefore carefully

balance the tradeoff such that the need to minimize credit application fraud risk (or other risks) does not result in an inordinate reduction in the bank's expected benefits and rewards from offering e-banking services (e.g., competitive advantage, operating efficiency, service quality, etc.). This poses the need for developing real-time, foolproof tools for use by e-banks in the front-end verification of online credit applications.

Repudiation Risk

Tools include:

- secure customer identification and authentication devices (e.g., personal identification numbers [PIN] and passwords);
- security systems that track and record transaction source and IP number down to the personal computer, laptop, notebook, mobile telephone, or other device used to initiate the e-banking transaction.

Reputational Risk

Tools include:

- prior and ongoing testing of e-banking systems to detect and avoid possible disruptions;
- testing of link-ups to other e-banking or e-business sites whose failures may pose reputational risk for the bank;
- issuance of disclaimers regarding failures or unethical actions of other e-business sites involved in an e-banking transaction.

To sum up, the e-banking risk management objective should be to maintain a risk–reward relationship in which the higher promised rewards generated by the increased efficiencies of e-banking are not wiped out either by suffering losses from accepting to bear inordinately-increased risks or by incurring excessive costs of detection, prevention, monitoring, testing, and other risk management and control tools used by the e-bank.

Economic Mismanagement Risk

Economic mismanagement risk is one of the important types of risk that must be taken into account by firms engaged in international business activities. It is related to but distinct from *political risk* (see p. 84). However, it may be considered as a component of *country risk* (see p. 11).

   Economic mismanagement risk is the probability that the government of a foreign country may, through corruption or ineptness, steer the national economy on a path that leads to economic ruin. As a result, firms from other countries which have business operations or interests in that country may suffer adverse effects on their profit, investment, and other goals.

   The most widely used indicator of *economic mismanagement risk* in a given country is the inflation rate. The persistence of "runaway" inflation—endemic in some developing countries—is an unmistakable tell-tale sign of high levels of *economic mismanagement risk*.

Environmental Risk

Environmental risk refers to the firm's exposure to possible but unexpected rewards or costs from interacting with the external environment. The definition of the external environment is very broad, encompassing the entire legal, legislative and regulatory environment, cultural and social norms, values and mores, and generally all pervasive external factors whose nature is non-specific to the firm, its products, or the industry in which it operates.

   Examples of *environmental risk* exposure include the enactment or modification of zoning laws, occupational health and safety regulations, pollution control laws, and so on. In some of these cases (e.g., compliance with pollution control laws) the firm's *environmental risk* exposure may result in additional, unforeseen costs, while in some other cases (e.g., a change in zoning laws which causes land values to go up), the result of this exposure may be additional, unexpected profits to the firm.

   Other examples of *environmental risk* exposure may arise in the course of the firm's operations. For example, the firm may unexpectedly become liable to the government, the public, or other outside parties such as other firms or specific individuals, as a result of damages or injury caused by the firm's personnel or property (e.g., involvement of the firm's vehicles in accidents, oil spills from tankers operated by the firm, etc.).

Ethical Risk

Ethical risk is the exposure of an individual or a firm to the possible dishonesty or lack of integrity of experts, consultants, specialists, technicians, and practitioners in professions which play an important (often legally required) role in guiding business decisions and investment behavior. Every situation in which the services of such professionals are retained may involve *ethical risk* due to the possibility that the professional may deliberately breach the code of ethics of his or her profession to the detriment of the party using his or her services, without the breach being immediately detectable by that party.

The following are examples of situations which pose a potential *ethical risk*:

■ An external auditor may act in collusion with the management of a company he or she is retained to audit and may submit an unqualified auditor's report of the company's accounts, in spite of irregularities in those accounts. As a result, other parties dealing with this company may unknowingly be exposed to *ethical risk* which may in time degenerate into various other kinds of risk. For example, a bank may approve a loan to the company, only to discover at a later point that its *credit risk* exposure (see p. 13) is excessive or that the company cannot repay the loan. Similarly, an investor may decide to buy the company's stock and later suffer losses due to misjudgment of the stock's *downside risk* (see p. 21).

■ An appraiser retained by a bank to estimate the value of property (e.g., real estate) may work out a secret deal with the owner of the property whereby, for a specified "bribe," the appraiser may give the bank an overstated estimate of the property value. Based on this estimate, the bank may approve a loan to the owner against a mortgage on the property. Later, in the event of default by the owner, the appraiser's *ethical risk* would have created excessive *credit risk*, possibly resulting in a loss to the bank.

■ A physician may, in return for a special fee from a patient, submit a "clean bill of health" on behalf of the patient, expressly for the purpose of securing an insurance company's approval of health insurance coverage for that patient. As the physician's report misrepresents the patient's actual health condition, the insurance company may approve coverage to the patient. As a result of underwriting an *uninsurable risk* in the belief that it is *insurable* (see p. 55), the insurance company would suffer losses on its policy to this patient.

The most effective measure for preventing or minimizing *ethical risk* exposure lies in the careful selection of professionals—and firms that offer professional services—based on their reputation and their track record of adherence to ethical standards.

Exchange Rate Risk

Exchange rate risk is the exposure of an individual, firm or financial institution to fluctuations (relative to the domestic currency or some other base currency) in the values of foreign currencies in which asset investments and their related financing contracts (liabilities) are made. Such fluctuations are continuous, and their effects may range from large gains to large losses on the base-currency value (net worth) of the initial investment made in a foreign currency.

Exchange rate risk may be classified, according to its outcome, into three types: *competitive risk* (see p. 9), *translation risk* (see p. 118), and *transaction risk* (see p. 115).

There are many possible sources of *exchange rate risk*, which may be exhibited through shifts in the supply of and the demand for a given currency relative to some other currency. When such shifts occur, fluctuations in the exchange rate are observed. For example, if there is an upward shift in demand for the US dollar relative to the Japanese yen, the $/yen (spot) exchange rate would go up. A downward shift in the supply of US dollars would lead to the same result.

Numerous factors may cause shifts in a currency's demand and supply. There are four main theories about foreign exchange rate fluctuations, and each theory focuses on a different factor or set of factors, namely:

■ actual (realized) inflation rate differentials between two countries (the

theory that exchange rate fluctuations are based on these differentials is called "purchasing power parity theory");
■ differentials in inflationary expectations between two countries (international "Fisher Effect theory"; see *inflation risk*, p. 45);
■ forward exchange rates (known at present) in relation to future (still unknown) spot exchange rates ("unbiased expectations theory"); and
■ differentials between the risk-free interest rates of two countries ("interest rate parity theory").

Relationship to Interest Rate Risk: It is clear from the foregoing that *exchange rate risk* and *interest rate risk* (see p. 58) are interrelated, and that the management of these two types of risk should be undertaken jointly, not independently. This is particularly important for commercial banks and other financial institutions.

Relationship to Political Risk: Another important determinant of *exchange rate risk* is *political risk* (see p. 84). All other things equal, the general rule is that demand for a currency increases (and the currency appreciates) with a decrease in that country's political risk components, and decreases (i.e., the currency depreciates) if that country's political risk goes up.

A seeming exception to this rule is the observed behavior, during October 2001, of the Afghan currency (the afghani) shortly after the start of the US and allied military campaign against Afghanistan's regime and the militants supported by it. Afghans reacted to the launch of the campaign with a run on the afghani, which caused it to appreciate by about 50% against the US dollar in less than two weeks. This presents a rare exception where the outbreak of war created positive internal expectations about the political future of a country, reducing its people's expectations about future political risk once the hostilities ended, and strengthening their confidence in their currency even as the military action was still unfolding.

Banks' Exchange Rate Risk Exposure

At a given point in time, a bank may have "open positions" in the various currencies traded by its dealing room. These positions may be "long" (when a currency is bought) or "short" (when a currency is sold). Open positions expose the bank to *exchange rate risk*. Specifically, a long position in a given currency carries a probability of generating profits if that currency appreciates, and losses if it depreciates. A short position is the exact opposite, with a probability of generating losses if the currency appreciates, and profits if it depreciates. Such profits or losses are realized when the position is closed.

An important function of risk management in banks involves the continuous monitoring, by senior management, of *exchange rate risk* exposure from open positions in individual currencies. For control purposes, banks specify limits on open positions in various currencies. In addition, close monitoring of overall exposure to *exchange rate risk* is carried out continuously. This involves not just open positions in any given foreign currency but also the total exposure through loans, deposits, and other assets and liabilities denominated in that currency, as well as those parts of the bank's equity (e.g., capital of its foreign branches) that are denominated in the foreign currency.

There is a wide variety of strategies involving derivatives (options, futures, swaps), which banks can use in hedging their open positions and their overall balance sheet exposure to *exchange rate risk*.

Expropriation Risk

Expropriation risk is a component of *political risk* (see p. 84) which affects a firm's investments in a foreign country. It arises from the possibility that a foreign government may take over the firm's overseas investments with compensation. Thus, *expropriation risk* differs from *confiscation risk* (see p. 10) in that the latter does not involve any compensation to the firm for the takeover of its assets.

The firm's *expropriation risk* exposure depends on two factors which work in opposite directions:

1. *Expropriation risk* (as well as *confiscation risk*) increases with the probability that a foreign government will take over the firm's assets. As a lower limit, if this probability is zero then there is no *expropriation risk* (and no *confiscation risk* either).
2. *Expropriation risk* decreases the higher is the amount of compensation that the foreign government is expected to offer, and the more promptly that compensation is expected to be forthcoming. For example, if the firm expects immediate and full compensation (equal to 100% of the market value of the assets exposed to takeover), then the *expropriation risk* is zero.

Fidelity Risk (see *Fiduciary Risk*)

Fiduciary Risk

Fiduciary risk refers to the possibility that an individual, firm, or financial institution, acting in the capacity of a trustee, may knowingly or unknowingly, in the course of managing funds held in trust, exercise discretion, make decisions, or take actions which fail to satisfy some applicable standard or "rule of prudence" against which such discretion, decisions, or actions are to be compared. *Fiduciary risk* lies in the possibility that the trustee (fiduciary) may become legally liable for losses resulting from failure to adhere to the "rule of prudence."

To varying degrees, all financial institutions have a fiduciary responsibility and are therefore exposed to *fiduciary risk*. Financial institutions whose primary function is the provision of security (e.g., insurance firms, pension funds) are governed by the "rule of prudence" to a much greater extent than depository financial institutions (e.g., commercial banks), whose primary function is to generate returns on deposited funds and capital. For this reason, elaborate rules and regulations in various countries bar insurance companies and pension funds from engaging in specific activities or investing in assets that are considered highly speculative in nature, and as such do not satisfy the requirements of prudence.

While similar rules usually apply to commercial banks and other depository-type institutions, these rules are not as restrictive as in the case of insurance firms, pension plans, and other fiduciary-type institutions. Nevertheless, in recent years there has been a marked and progressive change in the regulatory environment of banking, which has resulted in an increased emphasis being placed on the fiduciary responsibility of commercial banks. The multi-tiered definitions of risk-based capital and ensuing bank capital adequacy standards set in 1992 by the Basel Committee of the Bank of International Settlements (BIS), may perhaps be viewed in spirit as an expression of (among other things) this renewed emphasis on returning to the first basics of banks' fiduciary responsibility.

In many jurisdictions, fiduciary responsibility is gauged against a "prudent person rule." Typically, this rule stipulates that the fiduciary (trustee) must act faithfully and exercise at least the same amount of sound discretion and intelligence that might reasonably be expected of a person who, in managing his own funds, would give due consideration to long-term safety and probable income, rather than to speculation.

However, a movement is under way towards a new, higher standard: the "prudent expert rule." Indeed, this new standard has already fully or partially replaced the "prudent person rule" in some jurisdictions (starting with the US in 1974).

In essence, the "prudent expert rule" sets as a standard for prudence the actions that might be expected of an expert (not just any reasonable person) conducting the affairs of an enterprise with similar aims to those of the fiduciary being evaluated.

Financing Risk

Financing risk is defined as the exposure of the firm's earnings after taxes (EAT in the income statement shown below) to changes in the firm's net operating income (widely known as earnings before interest and taxes, EBIT).

For a discussion, in a financial statement framework, of the distinct and separate nature of the firm's operating and financing sides, see *operating risk* (p. 75).

In the following income statement, the firm's operating inflows and outflows are captured by the section that begins with Sales and ends with EBIT. The financing outflows (*I*) are relegated to the bottom section, between EBIT and EAT:

    Sales

  − Cost of Goods Sold (CGS)

  = Gross Operating Margin

  − Selling, General & Administrative Expenses (SGA)

  − Depreciation Expense

  − Other Operating Expenses

  = **Earnings Before Interest and Taxes (EBIT)**

  − Interest Expense (I)

  = Earnings Before Taxes (EBT)

  − Taxes (T)

  = **Earnings After Taxes (EAT)**

The firm's *financing risk* may be analyzed by reference to the effects of fixed financing charges (*I*) on the exposure of EAT to changes in EBIT. The "degree of financial leverage" may be used in this analysis.

Degree of Financial Leverage as a Measure of Financing Risk

The firm's *financing risk* can be measured with the degree of financial leverage (DFL). The DFL is defined as the elasticity of EAT with respect to EBIT. In other words, the DFL measures the percentage increase or decrease in EAT, in response to a given percentage increase or decrease, respectively, in EBIT:

$$DFL = [\Delta EAT/EAT]/[\Delta EBIT/EBIT]$$

where Δ represents a change (increase or decrease).

It can be shown (by substituting the components of EAT and EBIT in this equation, and then simplifying) that:

$$DFL = EBIT/(EBIT - I)$$

where I = fixed financing costs. Fixed financing costs are items such as interest expenses and financial lease expenses, which the firm has a contractual obligation to pay at specified points in time, regardless of the value of EBIT.

The main implication of the above DFL formula is that, all other things equal, the DFL (and hence the *financing risk*) of the firm is higher the higher *I* is, and lower the lower *I* is. For example, consider two firms in the same line of business which have the same EBIT but differ in their financing cost structures, as shown below. The DFLs for these firms can readily be computed using the above formula, and are also shown as:

	Firm A	*Firm B*
EBIT	$1,000	$1,000
I	$200	$50
DFL	1.25	1.05

Firm A has higher *financing risk* than Firm B, because the EAT of Firm A would increase or decrease by 1.25 times any percentage increase or decrease (respectively) in EBIT, while the corresponding increase or decrease in the EAT of Firm B is only 1.05 times the percentage increase or decrease in its EBIT. In other words, the EAT of Firm A is exposed to greater possible fluctuation resulting from ups and downs in EBIT.

This analysis provides a perspective on the relationship between a firm's choice of capital structure (financing mix between debt and equity) and its *financing risk*. If the firm uses a high level of debt financing (liabilities) relative to equity financing (net worth), then the firm will have a high level of contractually fixed financing costs (I) which must be paid out of EBIT. Accordingly, the *financing risk* borne by the shareholders (who only receive the residual EAT) will be high, and their expected return on equity must be commensurately high.

Foreign Exchange Rate Risk (see *Exchange Rate Risk*, p. 32)

Foreseeable Risk

Foreseeable risk is primarily a legal definition derived from the concept of "foreseeability." Accordingly, a *foreseeable risk* is any risk whose consequences can reasonably be expected to occur, by a person of ordinary prudence.

In many jurisdictions, a party's liability for damages arising from a breach of a contract, for injuries arising from negligence of tort duties, and for other similar consequences of his actions, is limited to the foreseeable consequences of those actions, as defined by the concept of *foreseeable risk*.

Related concept: *fiduciary risk* (p. 35).

Fraud Risk (see *Security Risk,* p. 92)

Fundamental Risks

The term *fundamental risk* is used to describe various types of risk whose scale and consequences are so far-reaching as to affect entire groups of people. Thus, *fundamental risks* are impersonal in nature, and any person affected by such risks is exposed to losses that do not arise from that person's own individual choice or behavior, but from events beyond his or her control. Examples of such events include natural disasters (earthquakes, floods), political and social developments (wars, riots, civil unrest), economy-wide phenomena (inflation, unemployment), industry-wide phenomena (occupational hazard), and so on.

Fundamental risks are to be contrasted with and distinguished from *particular risks* (see p. 79), which affect only specific individuals rather than entire groups. Because of their impersonal origins and their pervasive, far-reaching nature, *fundamental risks* are considered to be largely a social burden rather than an individual responsibility. This view provides the rationale for various social insurance programs, such as unemployment insurance, government-funded pension plans and health-care plans, disaster-relief plans, and so on.

Increasingly, however, this view of *fundamental risks* as a social burden is being relaxed, and the coverage offered by many social insurance programs in various countries is now being reduced, with the burden being gradually shifted to individuals. More and more, individuals are expected to take responsibility for managing some of the risks which for a long time were viewed as *fundamental risks*. In some cases (e.g., universal government-funded pension plans and health-care plans), the move towards privatization may result in the eventual dismantling of social insurance programs and their replacement, at each individual's option, with private insurance purchased by the individual. Thus, individuals are increasingly expected to make their own choices regarding the management of such risks, whether it be through buying private insurance coverage, taking steps to reduce or prevent losses from such risks, or by using other methods.

In short, many risks previously viewed as *fundamental risks* are now undergoing a definitional evolution and emerging either as hybrids (retaining some aspects of *fundamental risks* but also having some characteristics of *particular risks*), or as *particular risks* outright.

Growth Risk

Growth rates, patterns, trends and expectations are key indicators used in economic and financial analysis at both the macro and micro levels. Growth risk arises from the uncertain nature of the components or determinants of change in the value or quantity being analyzed. Thus, for a given economic or financial variable, growth risk measurement and management requires an understanding of the growth drivers specific to that variable, as illustrated in the examples below.

Economic Growth Risk

A widely used approach in the analysis of economic growth is the use of the "growth-accounting equation." For an economy utilizing n factors of production, this equation states that:

Total output growth rate = (Growth rate in factor 1)

     $\times$ (Factor 1's share of national income)

     $+$ (Growth rate in factor 2) $\times$ (Factor 2's share of national income)

     $+ \cdots +$ (Growth rate in factor n) $\times$ (Factor n's share of national income)

     $+$ Rate of technological innovation

Using a simplified example with two factors of production, labor (L) and capital (K), whose expected growth rates over a future period are $g_L = 1\%$ and $g_K = 0.5\%$ respectively, and assuming these two factors' shares of (i.e., their contributions to) national income are $w_L = 70\%$ and $w_K = 30\%$ respectively, with the rate of technological innovation g_{TECH}, expected to be 0.75%, economic growth, measured by this economy's expected total output growth rate (g_O) using the growth-accounting equation stated above, is:

$$g_O = (g_L)(w_L) + (g_K)(w_K) + g_{TECH}$$
$$= (0.01)(0.70) + (0.005)(0.30) + 0.0075$$
$$= 0.0160 \text{ or } 1.60\%$$

Growth risk may result from uncertainty about any of the determinants of g_O in the right-hand side. For example, if the actual rate of growth in the labor force is 1.1% (i.e., higher than the expected g_L of 1%); if the rate of capital deepening is lower than expected, resulting in an actual g_K of 0.2% instead of 0.5%; and if the actual rate of technological innovation is only 0.25% instead of the expected g_{TECH} of 0.75%, then the actual growth rate in total output would be:

$$g_O = (0.011)(0.70) + (0.002)(0.30) + 0.0025 = 0.0108$$

or only 1.08% instead of the expected 1.60%.

The preceding example underscores the importance of accurate forecasting and measurement of each growth determinant in the right-hand side of the equation above. It also sheds light on the manner in which key economic policy initiatives, such as reducing the unemployment rate (increasing g_L), stimulating capital expenditures (increasing g_K) instead of consumption spending, and providing incentives for investment in research and development (increasing g_{TECH}) can be instrumental in the management of economic growth risk.

Revenue Growth Risk for the Business Firm

At the microeconomic level, the process of profit maximization begins with generating revenue from sales and achieving continual sales growth. A firm's revenue (S_0) from selling a given quantity (Q_0) of a product or service at a given unit price (P_0) is:

$$S_0 = P_0 \times Q_0$$

Similarly, the firm's expected sales revenue at the end of a future period, say one year, is:

$$S_1 = P_1 \times Q_1$$

Thus, the firm's expected revenue growth rate is:

$$g_1 = (S_1 - S_0)/S_0$$

Sales revenue growth risk arises from the fact that the firm does not know the sign and magnitude of g_1 with certainty. The actual g_1 may turn out to be positive, zero, or negative, depending on actual sales during that period. The condition for achieving positive sales growth during a future period is an obvious one: sales must increase from their present level; i.e.:

$$g_1 > 0 \quad \text{if } S_1 > S_0$$

Substituting the values of S_1 and S_0, the condition for achieving positive sales growth becomes:

$$P_1 \times Q_1 > P_0 \times Q_0$$

All other things equal, for a normal product or service an increase in the unit price would cause a drop in the quantity demanded and hence in the number of units the firm is able to sell. A reduction in the unit price would have the opposite effect on the quantity demanded and sold. There are two possible ways in which such a change in unit price would satisfy the preceding condition ($P_1 \times Q_1 > P_0 \times Q_0$) and generate positive sales revenue growth ($g_1 > 0$). This can be illustrated with a simple example assuming $P_0 = \$10$ and $Q_0 = 100$ units.

Scenario 1: An Increase in Unit Price

Assume the firm increases the unit price to $P_1 = \$11$ and as a result customers reduce their purchases of the product and the quantity sold drops to $Q_1 = 95$ units. In spite of this decrease in quantity sold, the condition for revenue growth to be positive is still satisfied, since:

$$(P_1 \times Q_1 = \$11 \times 95 = \$1{,}045) > (P_0 \times Q_0 = \$10 \times 100 = \$1{,}000)$$

Sales revenue growth in this case will be:

$$g_1 = (\$1{,}045 - \$1{,}000)/\$1{,}000 = 0.0450 = 4.50\%$$

The reason is that the *percentage* increase in unit price, ($\$11 - \$10)/\$10 = 0.10$ or 10%, is greater than the *percentage* decrease in quantity sold, (100 units $-$ 95 units)/100 units $= 0.05$ or 5%. Thus the unit price increase is the dominant effect on sales revenue, resulting in a revenue growth rate of 4.50%.

Such a product or service is said to be *price-inelastic*. For such products and services, typically sold by few sellers or having few substitutes, the firm can apply a policy of price increases without fearing a possible drop in sales revenue.

Scenario 2: A Decrease in Unit Price

Now assume the firm reduces the unit price to $P_1 = \$9$ and as a result customers increase their purchases of the product and the quantity sold rises to $Q_1 = 115$ units. Although the selling price has decreased, revenue growth will be positive, since:

$$(P_1 \times Q_1 = \$9 \times 115 = \$1{,}035) > (P_0 \times Q_0 = \$10 \times 100 = \$1{,}000)$$

Sales revenue growth in this case will be:

$$g_1 = (\$1{,}035 - \$1{,}000)/\$1{,}000 = 0.0350 = 3.50\%$$

In this case, positive sales growth is due to the fact that the 10% drop in unit price $[(\$9 - \$10)/\$10 = -0.10 \text{ or } -10\%]$ is more than compensated by the 15% increase in quantity sold $[(115 - 100)/100 = 0.15 \text{ or } 15\%]$.

A product or service which responds to a price reduction in this manner is said to be *price-elastic*. For such products and services the firm can apply a policy of price discounts without fearing a possible drop in sales revenue.

To sum up, analyzing the price elasticity of demand for various products can be a very useful tool for managing revenue growth risk and incorporating pricing policy into the firm's overall risk management process.

Capital Growth Risk for the Business Firm

The primary source of capital growth for business firms is internal equity financing through the retention of earnings. Inadequate internal growth may necessitate an increase in external financing through issuance of additional capital stock and/or bonds or other forms of borrowing. Capital market conditions and the contractual terms of external financing may be unfavorable to the firm, and the firm's inability to generate adequate capital growth internally may be a factor in making the providers of external financing (e.g., banks, bondholders) set unfavorable terms for this financing. Such terms may include a higher cost of borrowing, limits on the present and future amounts of additional borrowing by the firm, and other "negative covenants" which may effectively diminish the owners' and managers' control over the firm's decision making.

To illustrate the process by which internal capital growth is achieved, consider a firm whose capital equity at the start of a given year is $1,000, and assume this firm's policy is to retain 40% of its net income each year, the other 60% being paid out in dividends. If, at the end of the year, the firm has a net income of $100, then $40 of this income would be retained and equity capital would increase to $1,040. The capital growth rate would be:

$$g = (\$1{,}040 - \$1{,}000)/\$1{,}000 = 0.04 \text{ or } 4\%$$

Using b to denote the firm's retention ratio, and ROE to represent the incremental return on equity generated during the year, it can easily be shown that:

$$g = b \times \text{ROE}$$

Using this approach in the illustration above, b is given as 40% while ROE can be computed as follows:

$$\text{ROE} = \text{Net Income/Beginning Capital Equity}$$

$$= \$100/\$1,000 = 0.10 \text{ or } 10\%$$

Thus, $g = 0.40 \times 0.10 = 0.04$ or 4% as computed earlier.

The ability to express g in terms of b and ROE is important because it shows that the firm can use two policy variables to manage and control its capital growth risk. These are dividend policy and investment policy.

Dividend Policy: The firm's internally generated capital growth rate (g) is higher (and its capital growth risk is lower) the higher the retention ratio (b) is. All other things equal (including ROE), to increase g the firm must reduce its dividend payout ratio.

Investment Policy: The firm's internally generated capital growth rate is higher and its capital growth risk is lower the higher the incremental ROE is. This points to the importance of maintaining the firm's competitive advantage and its ability (through research and development, innovation and inventiveness) to identify and invest in new, profitable opportunities that are expected to generate a high incremental ROE for the shareholders. Returns that consistently exceed shareholders' expectations would justify the firm's high retention, low dividend policy, and a high ROE coupled with a high b would make for a high long-term capital growth rate for the firm.

Hazard

Strictly speaking, the term *hazard* is not synonymous with the term *risk* in any of the different ways in which the latter term is used. A *hazard* is defined as a condition that may create or increase the probability of loss arising from a *peril*, or cause of loss. For example, a bank building is exposed to the *risk* of loss due to the *peril* of theft. The probable loss is made larger by *hazards* such as the existence of a back door with no alarm, an easily accessible roof with a staircase leading into the building, and so on.

This terminological distinction between *hazard* and *risk* may suggest that, in order to avoid confusion, *hazards* should not be included as separate headings in a work on *risk* in its many shapes, forms, and varieties. Nevertheless, while recognizing this distinction, three types of *hazard* are discussed below (see *moral hazard*, p. 71; *morale hazard*, p. 73; and *occupational hazard*, p. 75) in view of their significance to the field of risk management in general and to the insurance industry in particular.

Ideally Insurable Risks (see *Insurable Risks,* p. 55)

Inflation Risk

Inflation risk arises from the possibility that the general level of prices of goods and services in the economy, at the end of a given period, may be different from the level that existed at the beginning of that period. An increase in the general price level, as depicted by a rise in the consumer price index (CPI), would cause a reduction in the purchasing power of a given sum of money at the end of the period, while a decrease in the price level (deflation) would result in a higher purchasing power of that sum of money.

Changes in the general price level in a given economy may be the result of a wide variety of macroeconomic factors. For example, an expansion in the money supply, an increase in government expenditures, a reduction in income taxes and import tariffs, and easier credit terms that cause an increase in household consumption of (demand for) goods and services, may all result in a higher rate of inflation.

Anticipated Inflation and the "Fisher Effect"

Because investors need to protect the cash flows generated by their investments against *inflation risk*, the expected rate of return on any investment is set by incorporating an adjustment or premium for anticipated (expected) inflation during the holding period. For example, suppose an investor has $1,000 to lend for one year. If this investor requires a return of 4% on this loan, and if he does not expect the current price level to change at the end of one year, then he would quote an interest rate of 4% (the "real" rate of interest) to prospective lenders. The reason the investor does not need to quote an interest rate higher than 4% is that at an unchanged price level, one year from today, the proceeds of the loan ($1,000 × 1.04 = $1,040) would not lose any purchasing power in terms of the quantity of goods and services that the investor can buy for $1,040 at the end of the year relative to what that amount could buy at the beginning of the year.

By contrast, suppose at the start of the year the investor estimates that the price level will increase by 3% by the end of the year. In order to still receive the ("real") rate of return of 4% that he requires, the investor must receive a cash flow at the end of the year which is higher than $1,040 by an amount that is sufficient to protect the purchasing power of the loan proceeds against the 3% expected increase in the price level.

To achieve this result, the investor must plan to receive $1,071.20 at the end of the year, determined as follows:

$$\$1,000(1.04)(1.03) = \$1,071.20$$

If the actual inflation rate turns out to be as expected (i.e., 3%) then the $1,071.20 at year's end would buy the same quantity of goods and services for the investor as $1,040 would buy in the absence of inflation.

The preceding example illustrates the relationship between the nominal and the real interest rate, whenever the inflation rate is expected to be non-zero. This relationship, widely known as the Fisher Effect (in reference to the pioneering work of the American economist Irving Fisher in 1896), can be stated in a simple formula as follows:

$$(1 + \text{Nominal rate}) = (1 + \text{Real rate})(1 + \text{Expected inflation})$$

or

$$(1 + R) = (1 + r)(1 + i)$$

which can be expanded to:

$$1 + R = 1 + r + i + r \cdot i$$

Removing the 1 from both sides, the Fisher Effect is simply:

$$R = r + i + r \cdot i$$

In other words, the Fisher Effect states that investors set their required nominal (inflation-adjusted) rate of interest R by adding an expected inflation premium i to the real (inflation-free) rate of interest r as well as adding a cross-product term $r \cdot i$. In this way, the quoted (nominal) rate R provides protection against anticipated *inflation risk*.

Applying this formula to the above example, the investor will set a nominal interest rate of:

$$R = 0.04 + 0.03 + (0.04)(0.03) = 0.0712$$

or 7.12%. At this rate, he will receive $\$1,000(1.0712) = \$1,071.20$ in principal and interest at the end of the year, as shown above.

In periods of low inflationary expectations, the cross-product term will be negligible and may safely be dropped. This leaves $R = r + i$, which represents the simple and intuitive statement that the required rate of return which an investor quotes on a loan consists of a real (inflation-free or "pure") rate r to compensate the investor for parting with money, plus an inflationary expectations premium i to compensate the investor for anticipated changes in the purchasing power of the money he receives when the loan matures.

Unanticipated Inflation

In the preceding discussion, the focus is on anticipated inflation, and the assumption underlying the Fisher Effect is that investors can form correct expectations about inflation, which are captured by the inflation premium i. In this way, investors protect themselves against *inflation risk*.

However, this assumption must be re-examined by asking the question: What if the actual inflation rate i^* at the end of the holding period is different from the investor's expected inflation rate i at the beginning of the period? As a rule, there is no reason to believe that investors possess perfect foresight, and that their inflationary expectations will always (or even most of the time) come true. Thus, while the Fisher Effect equation shows how investors might deal with the anticipated component of inflation, i, it does not cover the unanticipated component, defined as $i^* - i$. (Note that $i^* - i$ may be positive, 0, or negative.)

To illustrate the effect of unanticipated inflation, suppose in the above example the actual rate of inflation at the end of one year turns out to be 5% instead of the anticipated 3%. The nominal interest rate at the beginning of the year, which would have protected the investor completely against *inflation risk*, is:

$$R = 0.04 + 0.05 + (0.04)(0.05) = 0.0920$$

or 9.20%. However, the loan was actually made at a nominal interest rate of only 7.12%, as computed earlier using the Fisher Effect equation. Thus, there is a remaining 2.08% (i.e., 9.20% − 7.12%) of unanticipated inflation, which the investor must absorb as a loss of purchasing power at the end of the year, due to uncovered exposure to the unanticipated component of *interest rate risk* during the year.

Obviously, if the actual inflation rate turns out to be lower than the anticipated inflation rate ($i^* < i$), then the uncovered exposure to *interest rate risk* would result in a gain in purchasing power for the investor at the end of the year.

Hedging Against Inflation Risk

As shown in the preceding example, fixed-income securities such as bonds provide investors with only partial coverage (if at all) against *inflation risk*, through the anticipated inflation premium i which is incorporated into the nominal interest rate. Thus, it is unanticipated inflation which poses the real challenge to hedging against *inflation risk*.

Common Stocks vs. Conventional Bonds

There is a growing variety of instruments and methods that can be used, with varying degrees of success, in hedging against *inflation risk*. In general, common stocks have demonstrated a much greater effectiveness in providing inflation protection than preferred stocks, straight bonds, and other conventional fixed-income securities. The reason is that firms (depending, of course, on their competitive position) can usually pass on at least part of actual inflation—whether anticipated or not—to their customers in the form of higher prices for goods and services. In this manner, firms' net income (available ultimately to common shareholders) is partially or completely protected against *inflation risk* while, in contrast, holders of preferred shares and bonds receive a fixed nominal rate of return regardless of the actual inflation rate.

Inflation Indexing of Pension Benefits

In Canada, the USA, and some European countries, there has recently been growing interest in providing inflation protection to pension plan beneficiaries, through the partial or complete indexing of pension benefit payments to the actual inflation rate. These indexing proposals would have the pension payments periodically adjusted upward or downward by all or part of the actual inflation rate during each period.

However, such proposals raise the politically and socially controversial issue of intergenerational transfer of *inflation risk*. Specifically, pension indexing would have the government play the role of underwriter of *inflation risk* to one generation (the retirees), with the "premiums" for this "insurance" being paid by another generation (the young, or the active workforce). With an upward long-term trend in the general price level, the government collects positive "premiums" from each successive younger generation, in the form of higher taxes or larger mandatory pension-fund contributions (deducted from salaries), which the government then uses to finance the higher (inflation-indexed) pension benefits payable to the retired older generation. The controversy over such intergenerational transfers of wealth is expected to grow, with populations becoming older and older due to increasing life expectancies and diminishing birth rates in most developed countries. The reason these demographic changes are expected to pose an increasingly difficult economic problem is that the active workforce providing the tax base and/or contribution base for funding the growing pension indexing burden is expected to decrease relative to a progressively aging population.

Inflation-indexed Bonds and Notes

Investors in several developed countries can also seek protection from *inflation risk* by purchasing various inflation-indexed instruments. In the USA, for example, the Federal Home Loan Bank (a government-sponsored system which provides residential mortgage financing) recently offered a large issue of long-term inflation-indexed bonds. Other issues of inflation-indexed bonds and notes have also been offered by the Tennessee Valley Authority (the largest electricity provider in the USA) and by the US Department of Treasury.

The concept of inflation-indexed bonds dates back to 1780. Such bonds have been available for a long time in several countries including the USA, UK, Canada, Sweden and New Zealand. The mechanics of inflation-indexed bonds involve indexing the principal (face value) of the bond to the CPI, such that the fixed coupon rate is periodically multiplied by an inflation-adjusted principal amount. In this manner, the bond pays coupon interest at the fixed coupon rate plus the actual inflation rate as measured by the CPI. Typically, the fixed coupon rate is set at 3% to 4%, which is the approximate range of the long-term real interest rate.

CPI Futures Contracts

Finally, it is worth noting that the growing availability of inflation-indexed bonds is now generating renewed interest in CPI futures contracts, which were first introduced with limited success in the mid-1980s. CPI futures would open up new opportunities both for speculating on price-level changes and for hedging against *inflation risk*.

Information Systems Risk

In the late 20th century, financial institutions and markets (and business firms in every aspect of their activities) were thoroughly pervaded by the rapid advances in electronic computing, information, and telecommunications technology. Concomitantly, the accelerating pace of globalization and international trade liberalization have turned this firm-specific dependence on computer-based automation into an interdependence which affects all counterparties to a given transaction, whether these counterparties are city blocks or continents apart.

As the 1990s drew to an end, the approach of the Year 2000 brought to surface a problem, which at first looked like a minor technical oversight in the design of computer hardware and software. In the span of just a few years, this problem became a focal point of research and analysis and the source of much alarm to all concerned. The financial and business community, scientific and research community, government regulatory authorities, and makers and users of computer hardware and software quickly formulated strategies and made huge budgetary allocations to deal with what they believed were going to be enormous multidimensional challenges, far-reaching implications, and a multitude of new risks arising from the Year 2000 Problem (Y2K; also known as the "Millennium Bug").

Origin of the Y2K Problem

The Y2K Problem can be traced back to the convention—adopted since the earliest days of electronic computing—which represents the year with two digits in all computer applications and also in the hardware and software which constitute the environment for running these applications. In this convention, for example, April 10, 1954 and December 31, 1997 are represented as 540410 and 971231, respectively (year/month/day). In like manner, January 1, 2000 would be represented as 000101. The Y2K Problem was posed by the fact that in the last example, representing the midnight of the turn of the millennium, the first two zeros would be interpreted by the two-digit convention to mean the year 1900 instead of 2000. Thus, it was feared that all time-dependent computer applications still using that convention were going to treat January 1, 2000 as January 1, 1900.

Examples of the Expected Y2K Risks

Because of the pervasive nature of the Y2K Problem, the range of potential risks posed by this problem was believed to be extensive and varied, and more potential risks kept emerging with the in-depth exploration of the problem and the search for remedies to it. The few following examples illustrate the magnitude of the feared problem from a banking, financial markets, and business perspective.

Breakdown of Computing Logic in Financial Applications

The erroneous interpretation of January 1, 2000 as January 1, 1900 was feared to cause a multitude of computational problems, resulting in serious disruptions to normal business operations. For example, it was believed that computers might produce negative numbers in interest computations on loans, resulting in interest charges being treated as refunds to customers. Another concern was that interest computations might be based on 100 years for transactions that are open for only one day (December 31, 1999 to January 1, 2000).

Disruption of File Storage Functions or Total Loss of Files

It was also feared that the inability of computers to recognize the newest data on January 1, 2000 might cause them to be treated as old data, resulting in file retrieval problems or even erasure and loss of such files. There was concern that this might cause major, wide-ranging disruptions to normal business operations, encompassing, for example, interest computations, customer billing, debt collection, purchasing, inventory systems, payroll, and so on.

Customer-relation Risks, Legal Risks, and Reputational Risks

As illustrated in the above examples, the possible fallout from the disruptions that were expected to be caused by the Y2K Problem was feared to go far beyond any single institution to affect other firms and individuals doing business with that institution. A main concern was the potentially serious damage to customer relations and to the institution's reputation. Furthermore, it was feared that an institution's customers and counterparties which incur costs or losses as a result of these disruptions might initiate legal proceedings against that institution, further aggravating the damages already sustained by the institution directly from these disruptions.

Security Risk

The expected breakdown or malfunctioning of date-sensitive security applications on January 1, 2000 was also feared to cause a sharp increase in both internal and external security risk to financial institutions, business firms, and other public and private organizations. It was even thought possible that security systems might work against the people they were designed to serve, for example, by locking managers out of their office buildings or denying them access to security-code protected systems (e.g., PCs, production equipment, etc.).

Other Major Risks—Credit Risk, Payment System Risk, and Contagion or Systemic Risk

Computer and telecommunication system dependency has created common interdependencies among banks and other financial institutions, business firms, and other participants in the financial markets around the world. Although efforts were being redoubled and the pace was being accelerated in 1998–1999 to make computer hardware, software, and applications "Y2K compliant," there was still believed to be a distinct possibility that through failure to comply, nondetection of partial noncompliance, or compliance implementation failure, there would still exist some noncompliant weak links on January 1, 2000. The fear was that it might take just one weak link in the system to bring the adverse consequences of any or all of the above risks upon some or all of the compliant players.

Strategies and Action Plans Implemented to Ensure
Y2K Compliance

In the late 1990s, many simultaneous Y2K compliance initiatives and efforts were undertaken, separately or in coordination, by various government and regulatory agencies, industrial and sector-specific bodies (representing makers, vendors, and users of computer hardware, software, and applications) as well as individual firms. For example, a comprehensive compliance framework for financial institutions was put forth by the Basle Committee on Banking Supervision, in the document entitled "The Year 2000: A Challenge for Financial Institutions and Bank Supervisors" (September 1997). This document can be accessed on the Internet at http://www.bis.org/publ/bcbs31.htm

Insolvency Risk

One of the distinctive characteristics of all profit-maximizing enterprises (business firms, commercial banks, insurance companies, etc.) is that their existence is derived from equity capital, and their continuity depends on the continued adequacy of their equity capital or net worth (NW). Stated differently, a profit-maximizing enterprise must remain solvent in order to maintain its going-concern status. This means that at any point in time, the value of the total assets (TA) of the enterprise must never be less than the value of its total liabilities (TL). This condition is based on the following basic accounting identity:

$$TA - TL = NW$$

Accordingly, the business enterprise is solvent as long as:

$$TA > TL \quad \text{or} \quad NW > 0$$

Insolvency risk refers to the possibility that the value of the total assets may fall, and/or the value of the total liabilities may increase to such a point that:

$$TA < TL \quad \text{or} \quad NW = 0$$

Note that the above situation is implicitly based on the assumption of limited liability, as the value of equity capital (NW) in case of insolvency is assumed to be 0 rather than being a negative value. This assumption is true for corporations, limited liability companies, and other similar organizational forms of business which confer limited liability upon the firm's owners.

The debt ratio (TL/TA) is a useful indicator for the assessment of *insolvency risk*. In a solvent firm, the debt ratio is less than 1.0, and the closer its value to 0 the smaller the firm's *insolvency risk*. It should be noted, however, that the current market valuation of TA and TL, rather than their book (accounting) values, should be used in this assessment.

Insolvency risk poses serious and potentially catastrophic threats to any business enterprise. One important threat is business failure or bankruptcy. While the event of insolvency should not immediately be construed as leading to bankruptcy, this latter outcome may become inevitable if the firm's management is unable to reverse the state of insolvency quickly enough. The reason is that the firm's creditors, possibly after giving the firm's management a grace period during which they expect the firm to revert to a solvent position, would lose confidence and start pressing for liquidation of the firm in any possible way, including legal action.

Another difficulty that would result from the event of insolvency is that while the firm is struggling to revert to a solvent position, and when its need for additional equity capital is at its greatest, investors may be so disillusioned with the firm's prospects for recovery that new injections of equity capital are virtually impossible to come by. Furthermore, insolvent firms are legally proscribed from paying dividends to their shareholders, despite the fact that their profits during that period may be positive. This may further reduce existing shareholders' willingness to maintain or increase their equity holding in the firm, and may aggravate its already bad position.

Short of liquidation, the firm may undergo a reorganization at the behest of its creditors, with the latter taking control of the firm and appointing a new management team with a fresh mandate to turn the firm around. Alternatively, the firm may become an attractive target for a takeover, as other firms recognize the potential profits from paying a "distress price" to take control of the firm and manage its operations more efficiently and innovatively, so that the value of its total assets is eventually brought back in line with their true economic value, and the firm reverts to a solvent position (i.e., TA > TL).

In the case of a commercial bank, *insolvency risk* may arise from the possibility of losses on the bank's earning assets (loans, advances, and investments) and its off-balance-sheet positions. Such losses are absorbed by the bank's equity capital. However, if the losses are exceptionally large and/or the bank's capital base is inadequate, insolvency may result and the bank may require emergency funds from the Central Bank, without which the bank may collapse within a very short time.

Insurable Risks

The term *insurable risks* is used to describe a set of ideal conditions under which *pure risks* (see p. 88) lend themselves to the insurance device as a method of risk management. Sometimes the term *ideally insurable risks* is used to emphasize the ideal nature of these conditions, and to point out the fact that insurance may actually be available for some risks that do not satisfy all of these conditions. The availability of insurance in such less-than-ideal cases may be explained by the principle of compensation, under which insurers may consider the ample satisfaction of one or more conditions to make up for the partial or total non-satisfaction of other conditions of insurability.

In order to be an *insurable risk*, a *pure risk* must ideally possess the following characteristics.

Expected Future Loss Must Be Accurately Predictable

It must be possible to accurately predict future losses expected to arise from the risk, so that insurers would feel it is sufficiently safe to underwrite that risk. There are five specific conditions for this to be the case:

■ The law of large numbers must be in operation. The number of units (e.g., individuals, firms, property, etc.) exposed to the risk should be sufficiently large. In other words, the risk should be one for which it is realistic to assume that the law of large numbers is in operation.
■ Past exposure experience must be available. Enough units must have been exposed to the risk in the past, so that losses incurred from past exposure can provide a reasonably representative basis for accurately predicting the frequency and severity of losses per unit of future exposure.
■ Exposure must generate sufficient future demand for insurance. In order for expected future losses from exposure to a particular risk to be predicted accurately, actual future loss experience must be as close as possible to predicted experience. This requires that a

sufficiently large demand for insurance of that risk (i.e., a sufficiently large number of insured units) should exist in the future. For such future demand for insurance to exist, the risk must be of such frequency and severity that it is economically significant to a large number of people. At the same time, the potential loss from the risk exposure should not be so large as to make the insurance premium prohibitively high, in which case other methods of risk management may be preferred to insurance.

■ Exposure must be independent. The units should be exposed to the risk independently, so that the loss expected from one unit's exposure neither influences nor is influenced by the loss expected from another unit's exposure.

■ Exposure must be homogeneous. The risk should be such that the units exposed to it face a probability of occurrence (frequency) of the peril (e.g., fire) and a potential loss (severity) from it, that do not vary widely from one exposed unit to another.

Expected Future Loss Must Be Determinate and Measurable

The nature of the risk should be such that potential losses arising from it can be specifically determined as to their:

■ cause of occurrence (specific event or peril, e.g., fire);
■ time and place of occurrence;
■ estimated amount of loss.

The ultimate purpose served by this condition (determinacy and measurability) is to ensure that the type, nature, and financial extent of the potential losses arising from the risk are relatively difficult to manipulate, forge, or counterfeit. In other words, to be insurable, a *pure risk* should not present the insurer with more than a negligible prospect of *fraud risk* (see p. 39) or *moral hazard* (see p. 71) being borne out as additional, hidden components of the insurance coverage.

Expected Future Loss Must Be Fortuitous and Accidental

The risk must be such that the potential loss arising from it is entirely governed by chance, and is not a certainty. In other words, two subconditions must be present:

■ There must be a non-negligible probability that the loss will not occur, and the higher that probability, the more insurable the risk.
■ The potential loss must be outside the control of the party exposed to the risk (i.e., there should be no *moral hazard*, see p. 71).

Expected Future Loss Must Not Be Catastrophic

The risk must be of such a type and nature as to make it highly unlikely for most or all those exposed to the risk to suffer losses together and at the same time. In other words, potential losses resulting from the risk should affect only a few units (individuals, firms, etc.) at any one time, so that it is possible to spread those losses and share them with the many units which did not incur losses at the same time.

If this condition is satisfied, the insurer would avoid the problem of "adverse selection." This problem arises whenever insurance for a particular risk is sought only by those who have (and who know that they have) a higher-than-average probability of incurring a loss from exposure to that risk. For example, if most or all of the people who buy earthquake insurance are people living in areas where earthquake activity is frequent, then a serious adverse selection problem would exist. By contrast, mandatory automobile insurance does not pose much of an adverse selection problem, because its mandatory nature ensures a random composition of the group of people who take that type of insurance.

Interbank Risk

Interbank risk is a potentially important source of *contagion risk* (see p. 11) in the banking system. *Interbank risk* arises from the possible adverse effects that the failure of one bank may have on other banks.

In a balance sheet setting, the assets of Bank A may include claims against Bank B. If Bank B fails, then Bank A's claims against Bank B (i.e., part of Bank A's asset portfolio) may have to be written off as a loss. If the loss is large enough to wipe out Bank A's capital, then Bank A would fail as a result of Bank B's failure. A third bank, Bank C, which has claims against Bank A and/or Bank B, may consequently find itself in the same predicament, and so on. Thus, *interbank risk* may result in a "snowball effect" that poses serious dangers to the entire banking system.

There is a wide variety of interbank transactions that entail *interbank risk* exposure within the banking system, and many of these transactions arise in the normal course of the correspondent banking process. In most cases there are obvious advantages or benefits to banks, in the form of faster, more efficient collection, clearing, and other banking services. Thus the acceptance of *interbank risk* exposure by banks may be justifiable as long as it is reasonably clear that the expected benefits outweigh the risks.

Examples of transactions that generate *interbank risk* include the following:

- balances due from other banks and depository institutions;
- loans outstanding to other banks and depository institutions;
- other banks' acceptances;
- "repos" (i.e., securities purchased from other banks, under agreements by those banks to repurchase the securities);
- cash items in the collection process;
- off-balance-sheet items such as interest rate and foreign currency swaps.

In countries which have a mandatory deposit insurance system, much of the *interbank risk* exposure is in fact shifted to the deposit insurance agency. When *interbank risk* is high, the assumption of independence of the insured event (failure of any given commercial bank) is no longer valid, and the risk covered by the deposit insurance agency does not satisfy the conditions of insurability (see *insurable risks*, p. 55). This may pose serious challenges to the very solvency of the deposit insurance agency itself in the event of multiple, interrelated bank failures taking place in the same short time period.

With or without regulatory action by the Central Bank, commercial banks normally use diversification of their correspondent banking relationships to reduce their *interbank risk* exposure.

Interest Rate Risk

Interest rate risk is defined as the exposure of an asset or a liability to market fluctuations in the level of interest rates during a given holding period. The sharp and steady increase in interest rate volatility since the early 1970s has made this type of risk increasingly significant for business and financial decision making.

For assets and liabilities that carry a fixed interest rate, an increase in the market level of interest rates during the holding period will cause a drop in the asset or liability value, while a decrease in market interest rates will cause the value of such assets and liabilities to increase.

To illustrate, consider a new bond issue which matures in two years at a face value of $1,000 and pays a coupon rate of interest of 10% ($100) annually. If the market interest rate (the yield to maturity required by investors) at the time of issuance is also 10% per annum, then the bond will initially sell at its face value of $1,000 as shown below:

$$\text{Initial market value of bond} = \$100/(1.10) + \$100/(1.10)^2 + \$1,000/(1.10)^2$$

$$= \$1,000.00$$

However, if the market rate of interest on such bonds increases to 11% on the issuance date then the bond's market value would fall to $982.87, as shown below:

$$\text{Market value of bond} = \$100/(1.11) + \$100/(1.11)^2 + \$1,000/(1.11)^2$$

$$= \$982.87$$

In the opposite case, a decrease in the market rate of interest to 9% would cause the bond's market value to increase to $1,017.59, as the following calculation shows:

$$\text{Market value of bond} = \$100/(1.09) + \$100/(1.09)^2 + \$1,000/(1.09)^2$$

$$= \$1,017.59$$

Price Risk and Coupon Reinvestment Risk

The preceding example illustrates that the market value or price of the bond during its holding period is uncertain, due to the bond's exposure to *interest rate risk*. This exposure is defined as the *price risk* (see p. 86) of the bond, and is one of two components which together make up the bond's *interest rate risk* exposure. The other component is the *coupon reinvestment risk*.

For fixed-income securities such as bonds, the *price risk* and *coupon reinvestment risk* always have opposite effects on the investor. To illustrate, consider again the bond in the above example, in the case of an increase in market rates of interest (from 10% to 11%). In this case, the *price risk* component is unfavorable as the investor has suffered a loss of

$17.13 in the value of his investment ($1,000) in the bond. However, the *coupon reinvestment risk* component has a favorable effect on the investor as the coupon income from the bond ($100 each year) can be reinvested at the higher market interest rate of 11% instead of the previous market rate of 10%.

In the opposite case of a decrease in the market rate of interest (from 10% to 9%), the *price risk* component is favorable (the price of the bond has increased to $1,017.59) but the *coupon reinvestment risk* component is unfavorable since the coupon income can only be reinvested at the lower market interest rate of 9% instead of the initial 10%.

Duration as a Measure of Interest Rate Risk Exposure

Duration is a measure of an asset's or a liability's exposure to *interest rate risk*. It is a weighted average of the time to maturity of each cash flow generated during the life of the asset or liability. The weights used in computing duration are the present values of the cash flows relative to the present value of the asset or liability. For example, the initial duration of the bond used in the above example, at a yield to maturity of 10%, is:

$$\text{Duration} = [\{1 \times (\$100)/(1.10)\} + \{2 \times (\$100 + \$1,000)/(1.10)^2\}]/\$1,000$$

$$= 1.909 \text{ years}$$

Note that this bond's duration is shorter than its maturity (1.909 years is less than 2 years). This will always be the case whenever an asset or a liability generates cash flows prior to its maturity date. In cases where there is only one cash flow which occurs at maturity (e.g., a zero-coupon or pure discount bond), duration and maturity will be equal. Under no circumstance can an asset's or a liability's duration be longer than its maturity.

Once duration is computed, it can be used as a measure of the *price risk* or volatility of an asset's or a liability's value to a change in market rates of interest. For example, the above duration of 1.909 has the following interpretation:

■ If the market rate of interest (yield to maturity) were to increase or decrease by, say, 1% of its original level (10%) [i.e., by (1/100) × 10% or 0.1%] then:

■ the initial market price of this bond ($1,000) is expected to decrease or increase, respectively, by 1.909 × 0.1% × $1,000 = $1.909.

Clearly, the longer the duration is, the greater is the expected fluctuation (volatility) in the asset's or liability's market value in response to a change in the market level of interest rates; that is, the greater is the asset's or liability's exposure to the *price risk* component of *interest rate risk*.

Using Duration to Hedge Against Interest Rate Risk

More important than its use as a measure of exposure to *interest rate risk*, duration can be used (and is very widely used) as a cornerstone of hedging strategies against *interest rate risk*. Duration-based hedging strategies can be used for single assets and asset portfolios, as well as in asset-liability management by banks, insurance companies, pension funds, and other financial institutions. "Immunization," "contingent immunization," and "dedication" are among the most widely used strategies which apply duration as the basis for hedging against *interest rate risk*. Increasingly, financial derivatives (options, futures, swaps) are being incorporated into these strategies because of the great flexibility they provide in achieving the durations required for effective hedging.

An Illustration of Bond Immunization Using "Horizon Matching"

Perhaps the simplest immunization strategy, involving a single interest-sensitive asset (e.g., bond), is "horizon matching." This strategy consists of matching the horizon or holding period of the bond to its duration. To illustrate, consider a five-year bond with a 10% annual coupon payment and a face value of $1,000. Suppose, once again, that the required rate of return (yield to maturity) on this bond at its issuance date is also 10%. Because the coupon rate and the yield to maturity are equal, the initial present (market) value of the bond will also be $1,000.

The duration of this bond can easily be computed as follows:

$$\text{Duration} = [\{1 \times (\$100)/(1.10)\} + \{2 \times (\$100)/(1.10)^2\} + \cdots$$
$$+ \{5 \times (\$1,100)/(1.10)^5\}] \div \$1,000$$
$$= 4.169 \text{ years}$$

Horizon matching involves holding the bond for 4.169 years and then selling it, instead of continuing to hold it until it matures at the end of year 5. If this is done, then regardless of what happens to the required interest rate (yield to maturity) in the market, the investor will lock in the initial yield of 10%. To see that this is true, consider the terminal value that the investor will realize under different interest rate scenarios.

Scenario 1: No Change in the Initial Yield of 10%

$$\text{Terminal value} = \$100(1.10)^{3.169} + \$100(1.10)^{2.169} + \$100(1.10)^{1.169}$$
$$+ \$100(1.10)^{0.169} + \$1,100/(1.10)^{0.831}$$
$$= \$1,487.87$$

Scenario 2: The Initial Yield Increases to 11%

$$\text{Terminal value} = \$100(1.11)^{3.169} + \$100(1.11)^{2.169} + \$100(1.11)^{1.169}$$
$$+ \$100(1.11)^{0.169} + \$1,100/(1.11)^{0.831}$$
$$= \$1,487.98$$

Scenario 3: The Initial Yield Decreases to 9%

$$\text{Terminal value} = \$100(1.09)^{3.169} + \$100(1.09)^{2.169} + \$100(1.09)^{1.169}$$
$$+ \$100(1.09)^{0.169} + \$1,100/(1.09)^{0.831}$$
$$= \$1,488.00$$

In each of these three scenarios about interest rate movements, the terminal value which the investor gets from holding the bond to its duration is the same (except for minor rounding differences). This means that effectively, the yield realized by the investor under scenarios 2 and 3 is the same yield he would realize if market interest rates did not change at all (i.e., 10%, as in scenario 1). In this sense, the bond investment is "immunized" against *interest rate risk*, by following the strategy of horizon matching.

Other Measures of Interest Rate Risk

Besides duration, other measures of *interest rate risk* include "elasticity" and "convexity." These two measures (and especially the rather complex convexity measure) are beyond the scope of this discussion, although it must be noted that convexity is finding wider and wider application in various areas of the investment and financial services domains.

Intraday Credit Risk (see *Payment System Risk*, p. 80)

Investment Risk

Investment risk (also known as *cash flow risk*) arises from the possibility that the actual cash flows generated by an investment (e.g., a commercial, industrial, or real estate project, etc.) might turn out to be different from the expected cash flows estimated at the time the investment was undertaken. For this reason, the decision to undertake an investment should only be made after this uncertainty surrounding the future cash flows has been taken into account.

There are several methods for incorporating *investment risk* into the analysis of prospective investments and projects. In general, two alternative approaches may be used: the Certainty Equivalent (CE) method, and the Risk-adjusted Discount Rate (RADR) method. Both of these methods involve the use of the project's net present value (NPV) as a criterion for accepting or rejecting the project.

The CE Method

The focus of the CE method is on the expected future cash flows from the project. Specifically, each expected cash flow is multiplied by a factor α, whose value is between 0 and 1, in order to adjust the cash flow to what might be considered a certain (i.e., riskless) value.

The value of α reflects the subjective assessment of the decision maker regarding how much *investment risk* exists in the project's expected cash flows. Inevitably, such a subjective assessment will be influenced by the decision maker's own perceptions of and attitudes towards risk. Thus, the more risk-averse is the decision maker, the greater will be his perception of *investment risk* and the smaller will be the value of α used to adjust future expected cash flows to their certainty-equivalent values.

Once the certainty-equivalent (risk-free) cash flows have been computed, they are discounted at the risk-free rate of interest and netted against the initial cost of the project to obtain the NPV. If the NPV is positive, the project should be accepted.

The following example will illustrate the use of the CE method. Consider a project with an estimated economic life of 3 years, which requires an initial investment of $400 and is expected to generate net cash flows of $100, $200, and $300 at the ends of years 1, 2, and 3, respectively. Assume the decision maker is not highly risk averse and is willing to assign a CE factor of $\alpha = 0.9$ to each of the future expected cash flows. If the risk-free interest rate (e.g., Treasury bill rate) is 6%, then the project's NPV, using the CE method, will be:

$$\text{NPV} = (0.9)(100)/(1.06) + (0.9)(200)/(1.06)^2 + (0.9)(300)/(1.06)^3 - \$400$$

$$= \$71.80$$

Because the estimated NPV is positive, the project should be accepted. However, the result would be very different if the decision maker were more risk averse and assigned a CE factor of $\alpha = 0.5$ instead of 0.9 in the above assessment. In this case, the estimated NPV would be $-\$137.89$ and the project would be rejected.

The RADR Method

The focus of the RADR method is on the discount rate used to compute the project's NPV. The expected future cash flows are not subjected to any adjustment for *investment risk*; rather, it is the discount-rate which is adjusted upward, by adding an appropriate risk premium ($\lambda \geq 0$) to the risk-free discount rate, so as to incorporate the decision-maker's assessment of *investment risk* into the estimation of the project's NPV.

As with the value of the λ used in the CE method, the value of λ is also influenced by the decision maker's subjective risk attitudes and perceptions. The more risk averse is the decision maker, the higher will be the value of λ he will factor into the discount rate as a required risk premium or compensation for the project's *investment risk*.

Using the project above as an example, and assuming that the decision maker, not being highly risk averse, considers a risk premium of $\lambda = 1\%$ as adequate compensation for the project's *investment risk*, the project's NPV can be computed as follows, using a RADR of $6\% + 1\% = 7\%$:

$$\text{NPV} = (100)/(1.07) + (200)/(1.07)^2 + (300)/(1.07)^3 - \$400$$

$$= \$113.04$$

With a positive estimated NPV, the project should be accepted. However, if the decision maker were very highly risk averse and set the risk premium at $\lambda = 14\%$, then the project's NPV (obtained by using a discount rate of $6\% + 14\% = 20\%$) would be $-\$4.17$, and the project would not be accepted.

Finally, it is worth mentioning that the Capital Asset Pricing Model (CAPM) can be used to obtain a more objective estimate of the RADR, which can then be used in project evaluation. However, to use the CAPM it must be possible to estimate the beta of the project. An example on this application is provided under the discussion of *systematic risk* (p. 101).

Legal Risk

Legal risk is one of the risks of doing international business. It arises from the weakness, incompleteness, nonenforceability and other similar problems with a foreign country's laws and its legal–judiciary machinery.

Such problems increase the probability that the legal system will fail to provide adequate protection of physical and intellectual property rights, or remedies against breaches of contracts and other violations of contractual rights. As a result, such violations may become frequent due to the deliberate opportunistic behavior by local firms in that country in their dealings with firms from other countries.

In reaction to a high level of *legal risk*, business firms from other countries will become increasingly reluctant to engage themselves in long-term contractual relationships (e.g., joint ventures) or even to undertake individual business transactions with firms and persons in that country. This may put pressure on the local government to reform the legal system and provide more adequate safeguards against *legal risk*.

Liability Risks

The term *liability risks* is applied to a very broad category of *pure risks* (see p. 88), many of which are *insurable* (see p. 55). Private insurance coverage for this type of risk (together with *property risks*, see p. 87) is provided by specialized insurers who sell the *property-liability* line of insurance services (formerly known as *property-casualty* insurers).

Liability risk arises whenever one party is exposed to possible loss of present or future assets or income as a result of causing one or more of the following events to another party or to assets owned by another party, whether those events (torts) are caused by the first party willfully or through negligence:

- physical, moral, or psychological harm or injury to another;
- damage to or destruction of another's property;
- invasion of another's rights (e.g., rights of physical or intellectual property ownership and/or use).

Liquidity Risk

In general terms, the liquidity of an asset is defined as the extent to which, and the speed with which that asset can be converted to cash. *Liquidity risk* for an asset is the uncertainty surrounding its extent of convertibility and its speed of conversion to cash.

There are three distinct components of convertibility, which independently or jointly determine the degree of *liquidity risk* of an asset. These are marketability (see *marketability risk*, p. 69), term to maturity (see *maturity risk*, p. 70), and certainty of collection or quality of the payment promise embodied in the asset (see *credit risk*, p. 13).

Four scenarios can be used in analyzing *liquidity risk* for an asset.

Scenario 1

Both the extent of convertibility and the speed of conversion are high or fairly certain; that is, the asset can be converted to cash instantly, and with negligible loss or no loss at conversion. In this case the asset has little or no *liquidity risk*.

Loss at conversion is defined as the difference between the asset's net value and its selling price at conversion, plus any transaction costs incurred in order to liquidate the asset. Net cost is the asset's original book value less any accumulated allowances, such as the allowance for bad debts in the case of accounts receivable, the accumulated depreciation in the case of depreciable assets, and so on.

Scenario 2

The extent of eventual convertibility to cash is high, and is expected ultimately to result in little or no loss on the asset's net value. However, the speed of conversion is low due to the absence of a ready market for the asset, to inactive trading (thin market) in that asset, or (in the case of receivables) to lax collection policies by the firm coupled with negligence and bad payment practices by its credit customers.

In such cases, the asset has *liquidity risk* and this risk is higher the longer the expected time to conversion. The *liquidity risk* is made even higher by the possible need to engage in a search for prospective buyers during that time or (in the case of receivables) by the need to factor the receivables, as the resulting search costs or factoring costs must be added to the loss at conversion, defined above.

Scenario 3

The speed of conversion to cash is high due to the presence of a ready market in which there is active trading in the asset. However, the extent of convertibility to cash is less than 100% of the asset's net value due to a structural drop in the market valuation of the asset between the time it was purchased and the time its liquidation is being considered.

As this drop in value presents the holder of the asset with a potential loss at conversion, the asset has *liquidity risk* which is higher the larger the potential loss at conversion (notwithstanding the fact that speed of conversion is high).

Scenario 4

Both the extent of convertibility and the speed of conversion of the asset are low, in which case the asset has high *liquidity risk*.

In any business enterprise, there is a tradeoff between liquidity and profitability. Thus, a firm in which there is a relatively high emphasis on liquidity must normally expect to sacrifice some profitability as a price that must be paid (much like an "insurance premium") for the reduction in *liquidity risk*. By the same token, a firm which decides to accept a higher level of *liquidity risk* must justify this acceptance by ensuring that a sufficiently higher level of profitability is expected as a result of it.

Liquidity risk management and control constitute an important part of the financial management process in business firms. *Liquidity risk* is controlled through the set of managerial decisions affecting the current assets and current liabilities, widely known as "working capital management" (Net working capital = Current assets − Current liabilities). In this context, ratios can be used in the assessment of *liquidity risk* for specific current assets as well as for the total current assets in relation to the current liabilities. The most widely used liquidity ratios are shown below.

For ratios with higher value, the lower the firm's *liquidity risk*:

■ Current ratio = Current assets/Current liabilities
■ Quick ratio = (Current assets − Inventory)/Current liabilities
■ Cash ratio = Cash/Current liabilities

For ratios with higher value, the lower the *liquidity risk* of specific current assets (receivables and inventory, respectively):

■ Receivables turnover = Sales/Receivables
■ Inventory turnover = Cost of goods sold/Inventory

For ratios with higher value, the higher the *liquidity risk* of specific current assets (receivables and inventory, respectively):

■ Days receivables (or Average collection period) = 365 Days × (Receivables/Sales)
■ (Days inventory = 365 Days × (Inventory/Cost of goods sold)

In a commercial bank, *liquidity risk* is one of the most critical types of risk which, if not properly managed and continuously monitored, may result in the bank's failure. There are two sources of *liquidity risk* in a commercial bank. First, the pattern (timing and amount) of withdrawals by depositors is subject to a lot of uncertainty, particularly with demand deposits. Second, the pattern (timing and amount) of demand for loans is also subject to uncertainty.

Thus, the most challenging task of liquidity management in a commercial bank is the frequent, simultaneous forecasting of movements in the supply of funds (deposits) and the demand for funds (loans), and using these forecasts to draw up plans for matching the two sides in a manner that maintains *liquidity risk* within the limits set by management.

Market Risk (see *Systematic Risk*, p. 101)

Marketability Risk

Marketability risk arises from the uncertainty regarding the existence, breadth and depth of the secondary market for any given asset. It is a component of *liquidity risk* (see p. 66).

For any investor or firm, and particularly for financial institutions (because they deal mainly in financial assets rather than in real assets), an important concern when choosing an asset for inclusion in the investment portfolio is the existence of a secondary market and the ability to sell the asset in that market quickly, at a stable price, and with minimal loss or no loss.

For a long time, the traditional (unsecured) loan portfolio of a bank was a major source of *marketability risk*. There were two main reasons for this. First, there were no secondary markets for selling loans from a bank in need of immediate liquidity to another bank, firm, or investor which had excess liquidity. Second, the use of diversification as a method for risk reduction in the loan portfolio, while being effective for reducing other types of risk (e.g., *credit risk*, see p. 13; *maturity risk*, see p. 70), did nothing at all to reduce *marketability risk* because prior to loan securitization this kind of risk was common to all loans without exception.

Loan securitization is one of the most important innovations in commercial banking, which started in the late 1970s and early 1980s. In essence, it is based on a very simple idea: rather than following the traditional intermediation process of making deposit-based loans and bearing their risks, commercial banks can arrange to make nondeposit-based loans and sell them (i.e., shift their risk) to other parties. Typically, this involves the creation of packages of small loans which are then offered for sale to investors as large collateralized securities. The collateral may consist of mortgages obtained under the original loan agreements, and may also involve the assignment of some of the bank's receivables from other activities (credit card receivables, lease income, etc.).

Through securitization, the originating bank transforms itself effectively into an agent for the investors who buy the loan-backed securities. Besides the advantages of reducing the overall risk (including *marketability risk*) in its loan portfolio by shifting some of this risk to others, the bank may also generate fee income from these investors in return for servicing the securitized loans (i.e., collecting the principal and interest on the loans).

Finally, at the international level, securitization of loans outstanding to various developing countries (notably Latin American countries) was used with good effect by many banks in the USA and other industrialized nations as a method for dealing with the "Third-World debt crisis" of the early 1980s.

Marketing Risk

The term *marketing risk* is used to describe the uncertainty that surrounds the future demand for a firm's products as a result of numerous variables which affect this demand, but may be unpredictable or not entirely under the firm's control.

Marketing risk arises from unanticipated or uncontrollable shifts in any of the factors which affect the firm's marketing mix (product, price, place, and promotion). For example, a change in the legal or regulatory environment may affect a firm's or industry's product design, impose price limits, restrict the geographical market, constrain promotional activity, and so on, with unforeseen consequences for future demand for the firm's products. The firm would then have to adjust its marketing mix in accordance with such changes.

Similar effects on future demand may result from changes in consumers' tastes and preferences, changes in the level of disposable income of consumers, advances in technology, intensification of price competition, changes in the availability and/or prices of substitutes or complementary products, and a wide variety of other factors which, independently or collectively (through their interactions), determine the level of *marketing risk* to the firm at any point in time.

Maturity Risk

Maturity risk is a component of *interest rate risk* (see p. 58). It affects every investment, project, or security which has a finite life (e.g., bonds).

The essence of *maturity risk* is the possible fluctuation in the market value of an investment, project, or security, as a result of fluctuations in interest rates and other rates of return in the market. The rule is that, all other things equal, the longer is an asset's term to maturity, the greater will be the range of fluctuations in that asset's value in response to market rate movements.

To illustrate, consider two 10% Treasury notes which mature at $1,000. Note *A* matures in 5 years while Note *B* matures in 10 years. If the going market rate (yield to maturity, assuming a flat yield curve) is 10%, then the present market values (PV) of the two notes are:

$$PV(A) = \$1,000/(1.10)^5 = \$620.92$$

$$PV(B) = \$1,000/(1.10)^{10} = \$385.54$$

Now suppose the going market rate for these notes increases to 11%, reflecting a general fall in demand for fixed-income securities. At this higher required yield to maturity, the present market values of the two notes will be:

$$PV(A) = \$1,000/(1.11)^5 = \$593.45$$

$$PV(B) = \$1,000/(1.11)^{10} = \$352.18$$

The values of both notes will decline. However, the 10-year note (*B*) will lose a greater percentage of its value because of its longer maturity and greater exposure to *maturity risk*. This is shown below:

$$\% \text{ Change in } PV(A) = 100 \times (\$593.45 - \$620.92)/\$620.92$$

$$= -4.42\% \text{ (loss)}$$

$$\% \text{ Change in } PV(B) = 100 \times (\$352.18 - \$385.54/\$385.54$$

$$= -8.65\% \text{ (loss)}$$

Moral Hazard

Because of its potential to greatly increase the cost burden carried by insurers, the prevention, control, and detection of *moral hazard* are important concerns in every branch of the insurance industry. Indeed, the absence of *moral hazard* is one of the main conditions for insurability of any risk under ideal circumstances (see *insurable risks*, p. 55). In reality, however, "ideal circumstances" (or some of them) may not always exist, and insurance of various risks is often underwritten in spite of the presence of non-negligible *moral hazard.*

Moral hazard exists whenever there are conditions which increase the probability that the insured person or other persons will intentionally cause a loss or will increase the extent (severity) of a loss, in the hope of defrauding the insurer. Thus, *moral hazard* has its basis in the greed, dishonesty, unscrupulousness, low ethical standards, and other similar flaws or tendencies in the character of the insured person, or of persons other than the insured person who find themselves in a position to benefit from an insurance claim by or against the insured person.

Examples of *moral hazard* include:

■ arson (i.e., the insured person setting his own property on fire with the intention of collecting from the insurance company);
■ unwarranted or excessive use of services covered by an insurance policy (e.g., medically unjustified visits to a physician, or staying in a hospital longer than the period required for recovery or treatment);
■ falsification of claims for damages by the insured (e.g., inclusion in a claim report of earlier damages unrelated to the damages caused by a specific automobile accident);
■ deliberate under-performance, shirking, and absenteeism by employees who periodically (whenever they have been employed long enough to be eligible for unemployment insurance benefits) cause themselves to be fired from their jobs so they can claim benefits from government unemployment insurance schemes.

In other cases, *moral hazard* may arise from or be aided by the complicity of other parties who stand to benefit from deliberately increasing the severity of loss suffered by the insured. Examples of such cases include:

■ garage owners who charge excessive fees for repairs to cars damaged in accidents, and persuade the car owners to accept the "fudged-up" estimates, since "the insurance company will refund them anyway";
■ lawyers who seek (and often obtain) excessive awards for damages to their clients in liability cases, because they know that the defendant is insured, and their legal fees are a percentage of the amount awarded to their clients;
■ making unwarranted claims (e.g., patients claiming damages due to

alleged malpractice by a physician, when the claimant knows in fact that the allegation of malpractice is unfounded).

It is noteworthy that in the first of the three examples immediately preceding, the insured (car owner) is an accomplice in the *moral hazard*, while in the last two examples, the insured (defendant, physician) is unwillingly and helplessly exploited by others whose target is personal gain from the insurance company.

For purposes of control and reduction of *moral hazard*, insurance firms use character checks and references on their customers, much in the same way that banks perform character checks as a standard requirement of their account-opening and lending processes.

Morale Hazard

Morale hazard is similar to *moral hazard* (see p. 71) in that both are sources of potentially significant increases in the cost burden borne by insurers. For this reason, both types of hazard receive a lot of attention and are targets of control efforts by insurers who—spurred by increasingly competitive insurance markets—have grown more and more sharply aware of the need to attain the highest degree of cost efficiency and cost effectiveness in their operations.

Unlike *moral hazard*, *morale hazard* does not arise from intentional dishonesty or abuse of the insurance coverage by the insured or by other parties. Rather, *morale hazard* is an unfortunate by-product created by the insurance coverage. It consists of the possibility that the frequency and severity of losses incurred by the insured (and claimed from insurers), may increase due to the feeling of security by the insured. In other words, *morale hazard* has its basis in the possibility that insurance coverage may bring about an unconscious or unintentional reduction in the degree of care and diligence that would have been exercised by the insured person in the absence of insurance.

Examples of *morale hazard* include careless driving, resulting in higher and more frequent automobile insurance claims; unhealthy lifestyles (e.g., excessive drinking, smoking) resulting in higher and more frequent health insurance claims; non-vigilance and lax security, resulting in higher and more frequent claims under theft and burglary insurance, and so on.

   A widely used method for the control and reduction of *morale hazard* is the *bonus–malus* system, whereby the insurance premium for a given insured person is set and adjusted by reference to the periodic claims experience with that person. For example, car owners frequently involved in accidents giving rise to liability claims may have to pay higher premiums (malus) to remain insured in future periods, while premiums may be reduced (bonus) for those who do not submit any claims during a given period.

Nondiversifiable Risk (see *Systematic Risk*, p. 101)

Nonmarket Risk (see *Unsystematic Risk*, p. 119)

Nonspecific Risk (see *Systematic Risk*, p. 101)

Obvious Risk

The term *obvious risk* is a legal term used to determine an employer's liability, at common law, for damages claimed by an employee under an alleged breach of the employer's tort duties.

   An *obvious risk* is any risk pertaining to the place, nature, and conditions of work (see *occupational hazard*, p. 75), about which the facts were known or readily knowable to the employee at the start of employment.

At common law, the notion of *obvious risk* forms the basis for the doctrine of "assumption of risk by the employee" and the "fellow servant" rule. The latter doctrine and rule are among the common law defenses that may be used by an employer against an alleged breach of tort duties.

The doctrine of "assumption of risk by the employee" holds that if an employee, having knowledge of the facts regarding the unsafe condition of the place of work, and understanding the risks involved (whence the term *obvious risk* is derived) has nevertheless voluntarily entered into employment or continued therein, then the employer is not liable for any harm or injury sustained by the employee in the course of or as a result of such employment.

Under the "fellow servant" rule, an employer is not liable for injuries sustained by an employee as a result of negligence by a fellow servant. Fellow servants are employees of the same employer, engaged at the same level of employment, and held to assume the risk of negligence of one another.

It should be noted, however, that statutes enacted in many common law jurisdictions (typically named Workers' Compensation Acts, or WCAs), have made it possible for employees to initiate WCA proceedings for damages as an alternative to common law proceedings. In such cases, employers cannot use any of the common law defenses, including defenses that are based on the notion of *obvious risk*.

Occupational Hazard

An *occupational hazard* is any type of risk that arises particularly from a specific occupation, type of work, or workplace. Examples include the much increased incidence of certain diseases, injuries, or mortality among workers in some industries: respiratory diseases among miners; cancer among workers in occupations which involve exposure to radioactivity; electrocution among electric utility workers; and so on.

Operating Risk

Operating risk is defined as the exposure of the firm's net operating income (EBIT in the income statement shown below) to changes in the demand for the firm's products or services, as reflected in sales fluctuations.

In the study of finance, a business firm's financial management and performance are viewed as consisting of two distinct and separate areas: operations and financing. These two areas, and the separation between them, can be seen in numerous ways, both in the theory of finance and in the practice of financial management.

The accounting framework of the business firm provides the clearest distinction between the firm's operations and financing, through the key financial statements, as discussed briefly below.

The Balance Sheet and the Firm's Operations

The pure operating side of the business firm is reflected in the left-hand side of its balance sheet (i.e., in the assets portfolio). The nature and composition of the assets (and hence the firm's *operating risk*) is largely dictated by the firm's line of business (i.e., what industry it belongs to, what products or services it makes or sells, etc.). For example, a manufacturing firm requires a relatively large investment in fixed assets (plant, machinery, and equipment), while an educational consulting firm, which relies mainly on contractual human resources, may require only a very small investment in fixed assets.

Another factor which affects the firm's *operating risk* is the type of technology used in the firm's operations. This is also reflected in the asset side of the balance sheet. For example, a primitive, labor-intensive manufacturing process may be exhibited through a relatively small investment (valued at cost) in machinery, plant, and equipment, while a technologically advanced (automated, or capital-intensive) manufacturing process may be reflected in a large value of machinery, plant, and equipment relative to the value of the total assets.

The Balance Sheet and the Firm's Financing

The right-hand side of the balance sheet reflects the firm's financing mix; that is, the specific combination of debt financing (borrowed money) and equity financing (owners' net worth in the firm). This financing mix may consist of a large amount of equity financing and a small amount of debt financing (conservative), or it may consist of a large amount of debt financing combined with a small amount of equity financing (aggressive), or any other intermediate configuration of debt and equity financing.

Separation

The separation between the operating performance and the financing performance of the firm lies in that the goodness or badness of the operating (asset) side is intrinsic to that side, regardless of the specific mix of debt and equity used to finance the firm's operations.

The Income Statement and the Firm's Operations

The following simplified presentation of the income statement is useful for clearly visualizing the distinction between the firm's operating performance and its financing performance.

> **Sales**
>
> − Cost of Goods Sold (CGS)
>
> = Gross Operating Margin
>
> − Selling, General & Administrative Expenses (SGA)
>
> − Depreciation Expense
>
> − Other Operating Expenses
>
> = **Earnings Before Interest and Taxes (EBIT)**
>
> − Interest Expense (I)
>
> = Earnings Before Taxes (EBT)
>
> − Taxes (T)
>
> = **Earnings After Taxes (EAT)**

In this income statement, it is clear that the section beginning with Sales and ending with EBIT consists entirely of operating, and only operating inflows (revenues) and outflows (expenses). Thus, this section of the income statement provides the appropriate framework for analyzing the firm's *operating risk*.

In contrast, the firm's financing performance (and hence *financing risk*, see p. 36) must be analyzed by reference to the bottom section of the income statement, following EBIT, as it is here that the effects of the financing mix are captured. Specifically, these financing-mix effects are the contractual, tax-deductible I accruing to the firm's debt providers, and the residual EAT accruing to the firm's equity providers or owners.

Degree of Operating Leverage as a Measure of Operating Risk

The firm's *operating risk* can be measured with the degree of operating leverage (DOL). The DOL is defined as the elasticity of EBIT with respect to Sales. In other words, the DOL measures the percentage increase or decrease in EBIT, in response to a given percentage increase or decrease, respectively, in Sales:

$$DOL = [\Delta EBIT/EBIT]/[\Delta Sales/Sales]$$

where Δ represents a change (increase or decrease).

It can be shown (by substituting the components of Sales and EBIT in this equation, and then simplifying) that:

$$DOL = (EBIT + F)/EBIT$$

where F = fixed operating costs. Fixed operating costs are those costs (excluding I, which is a financing cost) which do not vary with sales (see the discussion of *break-even risk*, p. 2).

The main implication of the above DOL formula is that, all other things being equal, the DOL (and hence the *operating risk*) of the firm increases as F increases and decreases as F decreases. For example, consider two firms in the same line of business, which have the same EBIT but differ in their cost structures, as shown below. The DOLs for these firms can readily be computed using the above formula, and are also shown as:

	Firm A	*Firm B*
EBIT	$1,000	$1,000
F	$400	$100
DOL	1.4	1.1

Firm A has higher *operating risk* than Firm B, because the EBIT of Firm A would increase or decrease by 1.4 times any percentage increase or decrease (respectively) in Sales, while the corresponding increase or decrease in the EBIT of Firm B is only 1.1 times the percentage increase or decrease in its Sales. In other words, the EBIT (net operating income) of Firm A is exposed to greater possible fluctuation resulting from ups and downs in Sales.

This analysis provides a perspective on the relationship between a firm's choice of technology and its *operating risk*. If the technology chosen involves high fixed operating costs (F), then the *operating risk* will be high, and the expected operating return on investment must be commensurately high. An example of a technology which typically involves relatively high F is an automated production process, or a process that uses highly specialized human resources or contractual skilled labor whose salaries are fixed (e.g., unionized labor). An example of a technology characterized by low F is a primitive, labor-intensive technology which uses hourly or part-time labor, and thus maintains the operating costs largely variable with demand and Sales.

In this light, multinationals and other firms which relocate parts of their productive operations from developed countries (e.g., North America and Western Europe) to developing countries (e.g., Latin America and South Asia) may in fact achieve significant reductions in their operating risk through the replacement of relatively high F with relatively low variable operating costs in their cost structures. If their product quality (both actual and perceived) is not affected, and they continue to sell and expand their sales in various markets at more competitive prices, then these firms may achieve higher returns for lower operating risks, and their overall operating efficiency would increase.

Particular Risks

Particular risks are those types of risk whose consequences (e.g., damages or losses) affect individuals separately, and are not so pervasive (as in the case of *fundamental risks*, see p. 39) as to affect an entire group of individuals. *Particular risks* arise from personal actions or events that are under an individual's control, and are therefore considered to be the responsibility of the individual, rather than the responsibility of society as a whole.

A burglary at a home, a fire in an office building, or a car collision are examples of *particular risks*. Individuals exposed to such risks can buy private insurance, and/or take protective or preventive (loss reduction) measures, such as installing burglar or fire alarms and driving safely. However, there are no social insurance schemes for such risks in view of the fact that they are considered an individual burden.

Payment System Risk

Payment system risk arises in connection with bank wire transfer systems linking originators and recipients of payments. It is primarily a type of *credit risk* (see p. 13) affecting the financial institutions involved in this link (commercial banks, Central Banks, brokers, and other nonbanks).

Known commonly as *daylight overdraft risk* and *intraday credit risk*, *payment system risk* results from the possibility that after a paying bank has actually made payment to a recipient specified by an originating bank, the originating bank may suddenly become unwilling or unable to settle its obligation to the paying bank.

The most important wire transfer systems are:

■ the Fedwire of the US Federal Reserve System;
■ the New York Clearinghouse Interbank Payments System (CHIPS);
■ the Chicago Clearinghouse Electronic Settlement System (CHESS);
■ the Payment System of the Society of Worldwide Interbank Financial Telecommunications (SWIFT).

Payment systems may be classified into two main types, which differ in the method of settlement.

Gross Settlement Systems

An example is the Fedwire, in which the Federal Reserve (Fed) simultaneously debits the account of the originating bank and irrevocably credits the account of the paying bank at the same time that payment instructions are received from the originating bank. The irrevocability of the credit means that there is no *intraday credit risk* to the paying bank. If the reserve account balance of the originating bank is larger than the amount transferred (debited), then there would also not be any *intraday credit risk* to the Fed. However, if the reserve account balance of the originating bank is insufficient, but notwithstanding this the Fed completes the funds transfer (which it normally does, for reasons of maintaining the speed and efficiency of the payment system), then the resulting overdraft would pose *intraday credit risk* to the Fed.

Thus, if the originating bank fails during the day, then the Fed may incur a loss in the same way as any other unsecured creditor of the originating bank. In other words, the *settlement risk* of the originating bank is borne by the Fed.

Net Settlement Systems

An example of net settlement systems is CHIPS, in which the net difference between funds transferred to a participant and funds transferred by that participant through the system is settled once daily at the end of the day.

In such a system, the *settlement risk* of an originating bank is transformed, in effect, into *credit risk* to the paying bank, if and only if the paying bank makes payment to the recipients of the funds transfer before settlement takes place through netting between the paying bank and the originating bank at the end of the day. For example, if the paying bank has made payment to its customers (the recipients designated by the originating bank), but the originating bank fails on that same day before netting, then the paying bank will only have recourse to its customers (the recipients) through requesting that they refund the amount paid to them in consequence of the transaction initiated by the originating bank having come unwound. If its customers are in turn unable to make the required refund, then the paying bank must absorb the loss through a write-off against its capital. In the event that the loss exceeds the capital of the paying bank, the paying bank would also fail.

Such a sequence of events may trigger a chain reaction where the failure of the originating bank results in the failure of the paying bank, which in turn results in the failure of other banks, and so on. This component of *payment system risk* is called *systemic risk*, in reference to the exposure of the entire banking system to such a chain reaction. (See also *contagion risk*, p. 11; *interbank risk*, p. 57)

Finally, it must be noted that a growing variety of potential sources of *payment system risk* is being recognized by banks, bank regulatory agencies, and the international financial community. Examples of these sources include:

Time-zone Differentials

In 1974, I. D. Herstatt, a large German bank, collapsed at the close of business which coincides with midday in the eastern USA. As a result of the time-zone differential, banks in North America which had already made payments to Herstatt did not receive their counterpayments (worth a total of $620 million) from Herstatt, as the latter bank had already collapsed before the close of business in North America.

Stock Market Crashes

The closure of stock exchanges in the USA for one day in October 1987 caused a brief but serious interruption in the international payment system, giving rise to dangerously high levels of *payment system risk*.

Integration of Emerging Capital Markets into the International Financial System

As more and more emerging economies in Asia, Africa, Eastern Europe, and Latin America become integrated into the global economic system previously confined to the developed nations, the probability of unexpected failure in the payment system is perceived to be increasing at an alarming rate, as not only the number of participants in the system but also the incompatibility between participants' risk standing are increasing rapidly.

Perils and Natural Disasters

In August 1990, the New York Fed was shut down for six days by a power cut caused by a fire at a Consolidated Edison station. In 1995, the Japanese city of Kobe was devastated by an earthquake. In both cases, jitters were sent through the international financial system due to the unexpected and dangerously high levels of *payment system risk* posed by these events.

Performance Risks

Performance risks encompass a large variety of interpersonal or business situations, which may give rise to contractually binding or nonbinding obligations. These risks consist of the possibility of loss to one party, in the event that the other party under the obligation reneges or fails to perform.

An example of *performance risk* is possible failure by a contractor to complete a construction project on schedule. For this reason, contractors are often required to provide protection to the project owner by taking out a performance bond from a financial institution as a condition for being awarded the contract. Another example is possible default (see *credit risk*, p. 13) by borrowers to repay debts according to schedule. Lenders may seek protection against the latter type of *performance risk* by taking a mortgage on property, collateral, or other forms of lien, security, or guaranty from the borrower or a third party.

As the preceding examples indicate, *performance risks* are a class of *pure risks* (see p. 88) and are generally *insurable* (see p. 55). In the above examples, the performance bond, mortgage, collateral, lien, security, or guaranty may all be considered as forms of insurance provided by the party from which the *performance risk* ensues, rather than being purchased by the party at risk. The latter party should continually assess the validity, enforceability, value and adequacy of these forms of insurance against the potential loss that might arise from the *performance risk* of the first party.

Personal Risks

Personal risks constitute a class of *pure risks* (see p. 88) which affect individuals rather than business firms or other organizations. They are normally *insurable* (see p. 55), with each subclass making up an important segment of the life insurance market.

Personal risks arise from four events which may cause an individual to incur a loss of assets or income. These events are:

■ premature death;
■ illness or disability;
■ unemployment;
■ financial dependence in retirement or old age.

Private life insurers around the world provide a wide spectrum of products that cover these *personal risks*, separately or in combination. In addition, social security schemes and government-funded insurance and welfare programs in many countries provide varying degrees of coverage of *personal risks*. Individual and group life insurance policies, private and public health-care plans, pension plans, and unemployment insurance plans are examples of some of the most widely used vehicles for providing coverage of *personal risks*.

Political Risk

Political risk is the uncertainty surrounding the value of, or the stream of earnings or cash flows from an investment, project, loan, or other asset held in a foreign country, due to sudden or unforeseen political developments in that country. It arises from five distinct risk components:

- *confiscation risk* (see p. 10);
- *expropriation risk* (see p. 34);
- *war, revolution, riot, and civil commotion risk* (see p. 122);
- *currency inconvertibility risk* (see p. 16);
- *repatriation risk* (see p. 88).

Multinational firms, banks, and other business enterprises which have investments, loans, or other assets in various foreign countries, are faced with the need to continually manage their *political risk* exposure. The process of *political risk* management involves two key functions. The first function is *political risk* measurement; the second function is *political risk* reduction and control.

Political Risk: Measurement

In recent years, a number of *political risk* indices have been developed and have found growing use in the measurement, monitoring, and control of *political risk*. In general, these indices are composites of key factors that are considered to influence the level of *political risk* in various countries.

An example is Euromoney's "Business Environment Risk Index," which is based on the level of Eurobond market interest rates. Another example is Knudsen's index which measures *political risk* in terms of the variance between national aspirations and actual achievements in a given country. A third example is Haendel, West and Meadow's "Political System Stability Index," which is a composite of factors such as:

- the system of government and its processes;
- socioeconomic characteristics;
- the rate of economic growth;
- social conflict vs. social harmony;
- ethnic homogeneity vs. ethnic fragmentation;

- the government's ability and effectiveness in controlling civil disorder;
- the incidence of riots, general strikes, demonstrations, civil commotion, armed rebellion, and *coups d'état*;
- disparities in income and wealth distribution.

Political risk: Reduction and Control

A number of approaches to the management of *political risk* exposure can be used, either separately or in combination. The main approaches are:

- Diversification of foreign investments, loans, and other assets among countries whose *political risks* are believed to be independent or negatively correlated.
- Financing the foreign investment, loan, or other asset through borrowing in the foreign country, with the loan being denominated in the currency of that country. This has the effect of creating a liability that perfectly offsets the political risk exposure of the investment, loan, or other asset in that country.
- Buying insurance against the components of *political risk* attaching to a foreign investment. Such insurance may be purchased from specialized government agencies in the firm's home country, and/or from private insurers.
- Maintaining direct control of critical operations and processes of a foreign project. This may reduce some *political risk* components such as *confiscation risk* and *expropriation risk*, by enabling the firm to withdraw its personnel and prevent operation of its project by others, in the event of confiscation or expropriation. However, this method is believed to have limited effectiveness, as it is not ultimately difficult, in time, for foreign authorities to replace the firm's key personnel with locals who are trained for that purpose, or with other foreigners who possess the necessary technical skills.
- Undertaking foreign investments as joint ventures, with equity participation by the government of the foreign country or by private partners in that country.
- Limiting the horizon of the foreign investment by undertaking a divestment schedule with a phased transfer of control and ownership of the investment to locals.

Portfolio Risk

The sections on *total risk* (p. 111, especially the variance) and *systematic risk* (p. 101, especially the covariance) should be read as a prerequisite for understanding this discussion of *portfolio risk*.

A portfolio is any combination of two or more risky assets. *Portfolio risk* is the *total risk* of such a combination, as measured by the variance of returns on the portfolio, or Var_p. In the simplest case, a portfolio of two risky assets, *A* and *B*, may be considered. For such a portfolio, the variance of returns can be computed as follows:

$$\text{Var}_p = X_A^2 \cdot \text{Var}_A + X_B^2 \cdot \text{Var}_B + 2X_A \cdot X_B \cdot \text{Cov}_{A,B}$$

where each X represents the proportion of the portfolio that is invested in each of the two assets *A* and *B*, and $\text{Cov}_{A,B}$ represents the covariance between the two assets.

For an expected or a target rate of return on a portfolio (set by management), the most efficient portfolio may be formed by allocating funds to the available risky assets (i.e., selecting the proportion of funds, X, to be invested in each asset) in such a manner as to minimize *portfolio risk*, or Var_p.

The starting point towards achieving this result is to select risky assets which have the lowest possible association, or $\text{Cov}_{A,B}$. A low (and, if possible, negative) $\text{Cov}_{A,B}$, representing portfolio diversification, will clearly reduce Var_p in the above equation. Computer algorithms exist for selecting risky assets which have the lowest possible covariance, and then allocating the funds over these assets (i.e., determining the portfolio proportions or Xs) in the manner that would minimize *portfolio risk* and lead to forming the most efficient portfolio.

Prepayment Risk (see *Call Risk*, p. 6)

Price Risk

Price risk is one of the two components of *interest rate risk* (see p. 58) which affect bonds and bond portfolios. The other component is *coupon reinvestment risk* (see p. 13). These two components always have opposite effects on *interest rate risk*. Specifically, when there is a rise in market interest rates, a bond's market price falls, but the investor can reinvest the fixed coupon income at the higher market rates of interest during the remaining term of the bond. When there is a fall in market interest rates, bond prices increase but the fixed coupon income can only be reinvested at the lower market rates.

Because of their opposite effects, the *coupon reinvestment risk* component and the *price risk* component can be offset against each other, resulting in a perfect hedge against *interest rate risk*. For an illustration of such an "immunization" strategy, which uses duration, see the section on *interest rate risk* (p. 58).

Property Risks

Property risks encompass all events which carry a possibility of loss, to a property owner, of one or more of the following:

■ the value of property (direct loss);
■ the use of property (indirect loss);
■ the future income generated by property (indirect loss).

Such events include damage, destruction, or theft of property, temporary or permanent inability to use property, and other similar events.

Property risks constitute an important class of *pure risks* (see p. 88), and are generally *insurable* (see p. 55). There is a very wide array of *property risks* in different areas of individual endeavor and organizational activity. Such risks affect every owner of property without exception, and can result in the direct or indirect losses shown above. For example, in the event of an accident, a car owner faces the risk of losing the value of the car, losing the use of the car (having to arrange alternative transportation), and incurring additional expenses in order to arrange an alternative. Similarly, the event of a burglary at a warehouse owned by an industrial firm poses the risk of loss of the value of raw materials, the income that the raw materials would have generated for the firm through the sale of finished goods, and the additional expenses of replacing the stolen raw materials (e.g., placing a rush order).

Property risks, together with *liability risks* (see p. 65), form a broad area of specialization (property-liability insurance) in the private insurance market, and are underwritten distinctly and separately from life insurance.

Pure Risks

A *pure risk* is defined as any risk which can only result in a loss or no loss, but can never generate any gains to the party at risk. In other words, a *pure risk* consists entirely of *downside risk* (see p. 21) and does not contain any *upside risk* component (see p. 120). An example is the possibility of loss that arises from owning property, such as a car. Various events, such as theft or a road accident, may cause partial or total loss of the car's value. At best, such events may leave the car intact. However, such events (in principle, and ruling out *moral hazard*—see p. 71) can never generate gains to the owner of the car or of similar property.

The designation of some risks as *pure risks* is useful for setting apart those risks that are normally *insurable risks* (see p. 55) from *speculative risks* (see p. 99), which are normally *uninsurable risks* (see p. 119). Several types of risk that affect individuals or arise in the course of business activity can be classified as *pure risks*. These include *personal risks* (see p. 83), *property risks* (see p. 87), *liability risks* (see p. 65), and *performance risks* (see p. 82).

Reinvestment Risk (see *Coupon Reinvestment Risk,* p. 13)

Repatriation Risk

Repatriation risk is a component of *political risk* (see p. 84). It is one of the risks that must be taken into account when a multinational enterprise is considering plans to undertake foreign direct investment (FDI) in another country. FDI occurs whenever one or both of the following actions are taken:

■ a business enterprise (firm, bank, etc.) acquires existing property (e.g., land, buildings, machinery, and equipment) in another country, or constructs new physical facilities (branches, plant, factories, warehouses) in that country, in order to carry out business or commercial activities or manufacturing operations through a direct presence in that country;
■ a business enterprise acquires a controlling interest in a foreign company, by purchasing more than 50% of the total capital stock of that company, making the latter company a foreign subsidiary of the acquiring firm.

To a lesser extent, *repatriation risk* may also affect firms which have a minority interest (less than 50% ownership) in a foreign affiliate.

Repatriation risk refers to the possibility of restrictions being imposed by the foreign (host) country's government on the movement of earnings or invested capital from the branch, subsidiary, or affiliate located in the foreign country, to the head office or parent company in its home country. The possible effects of such restrictions are:

■ to prevent the parent company from withdrawing part or all of its capital invested in its operations in the foreign country; and/or
■ to force the reinvestment, in the foreign (host) country, of earnings generated from operations in that country, instead of the earnings being repatriated for reinvestment in the parent's operations in the home country or other foreign countries, or for distribution as dividends.

As a component of *political risk*, the degree of *repatriation risk* attaching to investment in a given country is influenced in like manner by the same factors that cause *political risk* of that country to increase or decrease (see p. 84). However, there is one political factor and one economic factor that must receive special attention in the assessment of *repatriation risk*. These factors are:

■ The foreign country's general posture regarding FDI. If a country is known to have a relatively unwelcoming attitude towards FDI, then that country is more likely to impose restrictions that create *repatriation risk* for multinational firms.

■ The foreign country's balance-of-payments position. If a country has a net deficit in its balance of payments, or if it has a shrinking balance-of-payments surplus, then that country is more likely to impose restrictions on repatriation of invested capital and/or periodic earnings of multinationals. The reason is that the stream of repatriated earnings would be reflected as an equivalent stream of balance-of-payment debits (outflows) which, in the long term, may far outweigh any initial inflows or credits to the balance of payments which may have benefited the host country when the FDI was first undertaken.

Finally, it is also important to note the differences between *repatriation risk* and *transfer risk*, which are summarized in a later section (see p. 116).

Resource Productivity Risk

Any business firm, regardless of its industry or line of business (manufacturing, shipping, merchandising, financial services, etc.), must acquire productive resources (factor inputs such as materials, labor, capital, land, and so on) and combine them so as to produce its output in the most efficient manner. *Resource productivity risk* is the uncertainty that may affect the productive efficiency of any or all of the firm's productive resources.

Examples of *resource productivity risk* abound, and the following examples in particular illustrate the wide diversity of sources of this risk:

■ A "wildcat" strike or walkout by workers may abruptly reduce or remove one of the key productive resources of the firm (labor).
■ A fire, flood, earthquake, or other "acts of nature" may destroy or damage the firm's machinery, factory, office buildings, and other physical productive resources.
■ Labor costs may change in a manner which makes it either more favorable (more efficient) or less favorable (less efficient) for the firm to use the labor resource.
■ The cost of raw materials may also fluctuate, and this may affect productivity in a manner similar to labor cost changes. In some cases, raw materials may become more costly, be curtailed, or become temporarily or permanently unavailable (e.g., due to higher

shipping costs, trade barriers, blockades, embargoes, wars, etc.), with adverse effects on the firm's productivity. In the opposite case, where the cost of raw materials decreases or raw materials become once again available (e.g., as a result of the removal of trade barriers or the peaceful settlement of a political or military conflict), there would be favorable effects on the productivity (efficiency) of raw materials used by the firm.

- Similar positive or negative consequences may result from fluctuations in the cost or availability of capital resources (debt and equity financing).
- Finally, rapid or unforeseen changes in the state of technology may prove highly detrimental to the productivity of a firm which uses old or obsolescent technology, but such technological advances may reward a firm which is a leader in research and development and technological innovation.

Risk of Loss (in Commercial Law)

In any transaction involving the transfer of goods from a seller to a buyer, *risk of loss* refers to the financial responsibility for destruction or damage of the goods.

The question that often arises in this regard pertains to the allocation of the *risk of loss*; that is, whether at any given phase of the transfer of goods, the *risk of loss* is borne by the seller or the buyer. In general, the answer to this question turns upon defining an event or a point in time at which the *risk of loss* is shifted from the seller to the buyer. Accordingly, the question of who bears this risk can usually be answered by reference to the contractual engagement of each party, especially the clauses that define the modalities of shipment and delivery of the goods from the seller to the buyer.

Risk of Loss (in Finance: see *Downside Risk*, p. 21)

Risk of Loss (in Insurance)

The phrase *risk of loss*, as used in a general sense by insurance practitioners, refers to various hazards, perils, unknown events, and contingencies against which an insured party is protected, and for which coverage is provided by an insurance policy.

Risk of Non-persuasion

In lawsuits and legal proceedings, *risk of non-persuasion* is the risk borne by a party which has the burden of proof of some claim, allegation, or similar issue. The risk borne by this party lies in the possibility that the proof it puts forth may not be sufficiently persuasive to the court as to ultimately result in a decision in favor of this party.

The "burden of proof" is the duty of the party who makes a claim or allegation to substantiate it in order to prevail in the trial. Depending on the nature of the case (criminal, civil, etc.), substantiation may be met by producing "sufficient evidence", "clear and convincing evidence", a "preponderance of the evidence", or "proof beyond a reasonable doubt."

Security Risk

Security risk is an important and often insidious type of risk which poses potentially serious threats not only for banks but for every business organization. It is, or should be, at the heart of the risk-management process of all firms, but it has critical importance for the banking institution in particular.

All business firms, including banks, may be viewed essentially as vehicles for bearing risks in order to generate returns, which ultimately accrue to the stakeholders. The rules of efficient risk-bearing prescribe that in order to accept any given risk, one should first look at the various alternatives in that risk class and select the alternative which offers the maximum expected returns for a given level of that risk. Equivalently, in attempting to achieve a given target level of expected returns, one must strive to minimize the risk subject to the constraints set by the target returns.

What is peculiar about *security risk* is that it can never generate any returns to the party at risk. Therefore, no business entity acting rationally should ever voluntarily bear or expose itself to any type or amount of *security risk*, no matter how benign-looking or small that risk may be. The target for every bank and firm should therefore be the outright elimination of *security risk*.

However, because we live in an imperfect world, it is unrealistic to expect that total elimination of *security risk* can be achieved. Therefore, unconstrained minimization of *security risk* may be a more accurate way of describing the hoped-for outcome of the best efforts of business organizations in dealing with this type of risk.

What gives *security risk* its special, critical importance to the banking institution is the threat it poses to a bank's capital. By its very nature, a bank is a depository institution, in which equity capital typically represents a relatively small proportion of the total financing sources. A primary function of a bank's equity capital is to provide an adequate cushion for protecting depositors against potential losses which might arise in the normal course of operations. Such operating losses are largely predictable, and high-quality predictions, which have a high degree of accuracy, allow the bank to exercise effective control over its total *operating risk* (see p. 75). Such control can be achieved through setting prudential investment policies and practices, and through sound credit management.

Accurate prediction of operating losses also makes for higher-quality financial disclosure, and it guides the bank's financing decisions and their timing. For example, it allows the bank's management to make sufficient and timely provisions for potential operating losses, in the form of special capital reserves. In this way, the quality of financial disclosure by the bank is enhanced. If necessary, the equity capital may also be increased in order to offset the effects of a prospective increase in operating loss reserves and preserve the bank's capital adequacy.

In short, the key principle of effective risk management, which is widely understood and applied to banks' *operating risks*, is "prediction and control." However, in the case of *security risk*, where the objective is unconstrained minimization, this key principle should be modified to "prediction and prevention."

To what extent can this principle be applied to security risk in a banking institution? How predictable is security risk? To answer these questions, one must identify the sources of *security risk* and the red flags that are instrumental in its prediction.

Security Risk: Sources, Significance, and Some Widely Used Remedies

A bank's *security risk* may be defined as the bank's total exposure to the probable misconduct, dishonesty, and deceit by internal as well as external parties. In the 1980s, a study by the Federal Deposit Insurance Corporation in the United States showed that events such as fraud, embezzlement, falsification, and forgery accounted for a full 10% of large bank failures during a twelve-year period.

Prediction: The Key to Effective Prevention

Banks attempt to minimize the attendant loss from such events by putting in place a wide variety of preventive measures and early detection devices. Such detection and prevention are major functions of internal and external bank audits, and an elaborate auditing system may be used effectively in this regard. Security devices, online teller systems at branches, and special training programs are also widely employed by banks in the detection and prevention of security breaches.

Prediction is the art and science of projecting future behavior by using relevant information about past and present behavior. While auditing systems and security devices are not essentially predictive in nature, they do provide a lot of relevant information which should be used as important input in any predictive (forward-looking) assessment of *security risk*. However, the prediction process itself is a judgmental, evaluative process which involves much more than the mechanical projection of past and present information. Predictive assessment of *security risk* begins with identifying the major factors—both quantitative and qualitative—which together constitute the root cause of *security risk*. Once identified, these factors can then be incorporated into the two important processes of evaluating bank applications and regular monitoring of account behavior.

What are these major factors—these *security-risk* indicators or "red flags"—whose evaluation and monitoring every bank should integrate into the formulation and implementation of its credit policy and operating procedure? Or, posing the same question in different words: What are the major factors which increase the probability that a bank's clients—new as well as existing borrowers and deposit-account holders—will engage in fraud, deceit, forgery, document falsification, and other actions which might pose a security threat to the bank?

The Red Flags of Security Risk

The red flags of *security risk* can be classified into four major classes, namely:

■ personal red flags;
■ managerial, organizational, and operating red flags;
■ financial and accounting red flags;
■ banking relationship red flags.

The applicability of these red flags depends on the type of bank client: individual or corporate.

Individual Clients: Personal Red Flags

■ Individual who comes in for a one-off or once-in-a-while transaction (no bank accounts or established relationship).
■ Lack of reliable or reputable personal references.
■ Character checks incomplete, or information not available.
■ Substantial discrepancies in background information, especially trade/reference checks.
■ Evidence of poor character (e.g., previous check kiting, forgery, or other fraudulent acts).
■ Evidence of poor self-control or compulsive behavior (e.g., habitual gambler, alcoholic, drug addict).
■ Person with a criminal record.
■ Secretive individual who lacks forthrightness; reluctant to provide information or documentation.
■ Unsettled, transient individual with frequent address and job changes.
■ Individual in a hurry, who pressures bank officers to cut short the normal approval procedures.
■ Previous check kiting, default, or personal bankruptcy.
■ Individual who has marital or other serious family problems.
■ Individual involved in tax evasion.
■ Failure to perform personal obligations or meet commitments on schedule (e.g., pay the rent).
■ Reputation as wealthy individual or "society person," but assets and liabilities not clearly defined and not easy to locate.
■ Individual whose employer and/or sources and amount of income are not clear.

■ Individual who has unusually high personal debts or financial losses relative to personal income.
■ Individual whose disclosed income appears too low relative to normal personal or family expenses.
■ Individual who appears to be living beyond his means.
■ Individual who is known to be involved in extensive market speculation (stocks, real estate, etc.), to such a point that a market downturn would cause him severe financial difficulty.
■ Individual who is known to be under undue pressures or expectations (family, work, social, etc.).

Corporate Clients: Personal Red Flags

Apply the relevant personal red flags to each principal and key manager, especially those in charge of banking relationships.

Corporate Clients: Managerial, Organizational, and Operating Red Flags

■ Evidence of fighting or feuding among principals, partners, family members, or managers.
■ Illness or death of principals or key managers (resulting in a possible breakdown of internal controls.
■ High turnover in key personnel.
■ Sudden changes in management or ownership structure (resulting in a possible breakdown of internal controls).
■ Speculative business decisions and tendency to take on business gambles and undue risks.
■ Fragmentation of managerial functions, lack of coordination, and weakness or absence of internal checks and balances.
■ Absence of clear lines or organizational structures which separate authority over bank accounts of the parent company and those of its subsidiaries and affiliates.

Corporate Clients: Financial and Accounting Red Flags

■ Poor or rapidly deteriorating overall financial position and performance (high *credit risk* may degenerate into *security risk*).
■ Failure to provide financial statements in a timely fashion.
■ Poor financial reporting and internal controls.

- Unqualified audit (auditor's *ethical risk*, see p. 31; possible collusion between firm and auditor to cover up risky or fraudulent activities within the firm, which may generate *security risk* for the bank).
- Sudden or frequent change of auditing firms, especially from a reputable firm to a little-known, obscure firm.
- Company retains different auditing firms for its major subsidiaries.
- Major unexplained or arbitrary changes in account names or accounting methods (possible internal fraud within the firm which may engender *security risk* to the bank).
- The presence, in the company's financial statements, of debt due to or from the company's officers, owners, or subsidiaries and affiliates.
- The presence of substantial "intangibles" whose nature or valuation basis is unclear.
- Gradual, or sudden and substantial increase in "intangibles".
- Presence of substantial capital reserves whose nature or purpose is unclear.
- Gradual, or sudden and substantial increase in capital reserves.
- Appearance of unusual off-balance sheet items whose nature, purpose and relationship to the company's operations and financing are difficult to verify.

Personal and Corporate Clients: Banking Relationship Red Flags (Deposit Account and Loan Request Behavior)

- Bank accounts/loans managed by the same corporate officer for a long period.
- Marked change in established patterns of checking account balances (either a sudden, sharp decline or a sustained downward trend).
- Sudden lack of cooperation or adverse or suspicious change in attitude, behavior or personal comportment of the firm's principals or managers.
- Marked increase in frequency of withdrawals.
- Onset of overdrafts, suddenly or gradually over a period of time.
- Presentation of checks for much larger amounts than usual.
- Presentation of checks bearing authorized signatures of principals or officers other than those who normally sign cheques.
- Presentation of checks written against uncollected funds (e.g., against checks deposited into the same account but still in the collection process).
- Marked change in timing of seasonal loan requests.
- Marked increase in frequency and size of loan requests.

■ Piecemeal loan request where completion of documentation is promised later.

The foregoing red flags are the basic ingredients for developing more effective evaluation and monitoring policies, in dealing with bank customer applications and account behavior. These red flags (and any others which might evolve out of a bank's experience) should be formally organized into a *security risk* checklist, with each red flag assigned a weight and a number of points on a *security-risk* scale. The weighting scheme for each red flag should reflect the bank's accumulated experience as to the frequency of security breaches and the severity of losses in which that particular red flag was a factor. The weighted points for all these red flags can then be added up, and the grand total can be compared to a critical value, set with reference to the bank's "best" accounts, and again determined on the basis of the bank's accumulated experience.

By integrating such a scheme into the evaluation of each and every bank application, and into the regular monitoring of account behavior, it would become possible to stratify the entire bank portfolio—comprising the borrowing as well as the deposit accounts—into *security-risk* classes. This would make for more accurate predictive assessment of customer-related *security risk*, and more effective detection and prevention, leading to the minimization of bank losses arising from this type of risk.

Settlement Risk

Settlement risk is defined as the risk that a financial institution originating a funds transfer through the international payment system, may be unable to settle its obligation to one or more participants in the system, after those participants have effected payment on the originating institution's instructions. In essence, *settlement risk* is a type of *credit risk* arising within the international payment system (see *payment system risk*, p. 80).

Sovereign Risk

Sovereign risk encompasses a major category of risk types and situations that generate the overall *country risk* (see p. 11) exposure of a bank, business firm, or individual investor, whenever they have loans outstanding or assets invested in a foreign country.

In the most extreme cases, *sovereign risk* may take the form of *default (credit) risk* (see p. 13), with one important difference: that the defaulting party is the sovereign government of a foreign country. Alternatively, *sovereign risk* may be in the form of *confiscation risk* (see p. 10) or *expropriation risk* (see p. 34), when there is a high probability that a foreign government will seize the assets of a bank, firm, or individual without providing any compensation, or with only partial compensation.

In extreme cases like these, there may be no legal avenues whereby the lender or asset owner can seek redress against the defaulting, confiscating, or expropriating party. In its more normal forms, however, *sovereign risk* may arise from situations that do not carry a high probability of default scenarios, and are not expected to result in an outright loss of assets or write-off of loans.

A common example is the inability of a lender to enforce negative covenants and other terms included in loan agreements, when the other party is not a domestic borrower but a foreign government. There may be little legal remedy or other redress for the lender, if a sovereign borrower breaches a covenant that bars further borrowing. As a result, the debt-service ability of the sovereign borrower may be seriously reduced, making the original loan riskier without providing any compensation for the additional risk by way of higher expected returns.

Specific Risk (see *Unsystematic Risk*, p. 119)

Speculative Risk

Speculative risk, as distinguished from *pure risk* (see p. 88), is a term applied to describe all risky situations that, in addition to carrying the possibility of loss, also carry the possibility of gain to the party at risk. In other words, *speculative risks* incorporate not only a *downside risk* component (see p. 21) but also an *upside risk* component (see p. 120) as well.

Activities which involve *speculative risk* are usually carried out in the expectation of generating a gain, although the person choosing to undertake such activities is usually aware that there is a chance of the actual outcome being a loss instead. The range of such activities is very wide, and includes all gambling situations and games of chance as one extreme.

Gambling is unique in that risk is artificially created and deliberately undertaken in the hope of gain. For this reason, gambling behavior may be described as *risk-seeking* behavior. However, the range of activities involving *speculative risk* consists for the most part of activities that are normally considered to be consistent with *risk-averse* behavior. Examples from business and economic life abound, and they encompass the entire entrepreneurial process by which capitalists (individually or collectively through the business firm as a vehicle) seek to maximize wealth through profit-generating activities.

An important aspect of *speculative risks* is that, with very rare exceptions, they are *uninsurable risks* (see p. 119). The reason may be that in some cases, those risks may arise from situations for which insurance is not required. However, in the great majority of cases, the reason why *speculative risks* are *uninsurable risks* is that they do not satisfy one or more of the conditions of insurability (see *insurable risks*, p. 55).

While the person or firm which deliberately accepts exposure to *speculative risks* can reduce that exposure through a variety of hedging and/or diversification strategies (i.e., insurance is not required), it is not usually possible to buy insurance against this exposure, since no insurance firm is normally willing to provide protection against possible losses arising from voluntary speculative behavior (i.e., the conditions of insurability are not met).

In recent years, an evolutionary trend towards providing insurance for some types of *speculative risk* has been observed. In one example from the USA, the purchaser of an asset, such as capital equipment, can buy an insurance policy which provides indemnity for the possible drop in the residual value of the asset below a specified value during the term of the insurance policy. In another case, protection against *inflation risk* (see p. 45) is provided by a life insurer through periodic adjustments of the face value of its policies to increases in the Consumer Price Index. A third example is that investors in some mutual funds may purchase insurance against losses arising from the possible drop in the price of their shares below the initial purchase price, at the end of a specified holding period. The rapid growth in derivative markets and instruments has been a major factor in enabling insurers to underwrite and hedge against such *speculative risks*, previously considered uninsurable.

Static Risk

Static risk is a term applied to describe those risks which arise from events or causes that are not related to economy-wide structural movements, adjustments, or corrections. The possible results of any *static risk* consist of the transfer of physical possession of an asset (e.g., due to fraud, embezzlement, theft, negligence, etc.), or partial damage or total destruction of the asset (e.g., due to fire, flood, or other natural perils).

Static risks and the attendant losses which result from them are viewed as being highly regular over time, and their occurrence is believed to be largely independent of fluctuations in economic activity. For example, losses resulting from fires are fairly regular, regardless of whether the economy is in an expansionary phase (recovery, boom) or contractionary phase (recession, depression).

However, for some types of *static risk*, this regularity or independence from economy-wide changes may not be as high as is generally believed, if due consideration is given to *moral hazard* (see p. 71), which tends to increase in periods of economic contraction. An example is an owner of a business or a home owner who—in bad times—deliberately sets the property on fire in order to generate badly needed cash from an insurance policy. Another example is the marked increase in fraud, theft, and other acts of dishonesty during periods of economic depression.

An important characteristic of *static risks* (cf. *dynamic risks*, p. 24) is that they do not generate any long-term benefits for society. The reason is that *static risks* are generally not linked to economy-wide corrections or adjustments (e.g., downsizing, layoffs, price-level adjustments, etc.) which are necessary and beneficial to society in the long term, although their immediate short-term effects may be adverse.

Systematic Risk

A prior reading of the discussion of *total risk* (see p. 111) is a prerequisite for understanding this discussion of *systematic risk*.

The *total risk* (see p. 111) of an asset, investment, security, or project, consists of two components:

■ a nondiversifiable component, known as the *systematic risk* (also known as the *nonspecific risk* or *market risk*); and

102a diversifiable component, known as the *unsystematic risk* (see p. 119; also known as the *specific risk*, *unique risk*, or *nonmarket risk*).

As an example, consider the market price of a given stock. The overall fluctuation in the stock price over time is represented by its *total risk*, and is measured by the variance or standard deviation of the stock price (discussed below). If one considered carefully the factors that generate this overall fluctuation, it would be possible to classify those factors into two distinct groups:

1. Factors which have a common (but not necessarily equal) effect on all risky assets, investments, securities, and projects, and are not unique or specific to any given asset, security, investment, or project. Examples of such factors include all economy-wide or market-wide factors (inflation, unemployment, political factors, the tax environment, and so on). Such factors affect all risky assets in the sense that part of the fluctuation in the market value of every risky asset (i.e., part of the asset's *total risk*) is due to these common factors. This part of the *total risk* is called the *systematic risk* of the asset.

   Another way of describing the nature of these factors is to consider two risky assets, say the common stock of an automobile manufacturer and the common stock of a foodstuff packaging firm. Obviously, there are big differences in the nature of these two firms' business activities, competitive positions, demand conditions, management processes, technology, and other firm-specific factors. However, regardless of how different these two firms may be, they will both be affected (albeit unequally) by changes in inflation, the introduction of new tax rules, the general level of demand and economic activity, and other market-wide (systematic) factors. Thus, if one combined these two stocks to form a portfolio (see *portfolio risk*, p. 86), the part of their *total risk* which arises from those common factors (i.e., their *systematic risk*) would not be diversified away, but would remain in the portfolio.
2. Factors which are unique to a particular risky asset, investment, security, or project (discussed under *unsystematic risk*, p. 119).

Measurement of Systematic Risk

Perhaps the most widely used measure of the *systematic risk* of an asset, investment, or project is "beta." Beta is a unit-free index of *systematic*

risk, whose derivation is based on the simple statistical concept of association or covariance between two random variables (see the example and
discussion under *total risk*, p. 111).

To illustrate the concept and measurement of the covariance, consider
two stocks, X and Y, whose possible market prices and probabilities
appear below:

X	Y	$Prob(X,Y)$
$1	$5	0.3
$2	$6	0.4
$3	$3	0.2
$4	$1	0.1
		$\overline{1.0}$

In this example, $Prob(X,Y)$ represents the joint probability of occurrence
of each pair of possible values of X and Y. It is also assumed, for sim-
plicity, that this joint probability is the same as the probability of occurrence of X and Y considered separately; i.e.:

$$Prob(X, Y) = Prob(X) = Prob(Y)$$

The means of X and Y are:

$$E(X) = (\$1 \times 0.3) + (\$2 \times 0.4) + (\$3 \times 0.2) + (\$4 \times 0.1) = \$2.1$$
$$E(Y) = (\$5 \times 0.3) + (\$6 \times 0.4) + (\$3 \times 0.2) + (\$1 \times 0.1) = \$4.6$$

The variances of X and Y are:

$$Var(X) = [(\$1 - \$2.1)^2 \times (0.3)] + [(\$2 - \$2.1)^2 \times (0.4)]$$
$$+ [(\$3 - \$2.1)^2 \times (0.2)] + [(\$4 - \$2.1)^2 \times (0.1)]$$
$$= 0.89\$^2$$

$$Var(Y) = [(\$5 - \$4.6)^2 \times (0.3)] + [(\$6 - \$4.6)^2 \times (0.4)]$$
$$+ [(\$3 - \$4.6)^2 \times (0.2)] + [(\$1 - \$4.6)^2 \times (0.1)]$$
$$= 2.64\$^2$$

The covariance between X and Y measures the association between these two stocks' price movements; however, association does not tell us anything about causality between X and Y. In other words, we cannot use association, as measured by the covariance, to make any statements about whether movements in X give rise to movements in Y or vice versa.

The covariance between X and Y can be measured as follows:

$$\text{Cov}(X, Y) = \sum [X - E(X)] \cdot [Y - E(Y)] \cdot \text{Prob}(X, Y)$$

Thus, using the above data for X and Y:

$$\begin{aligned}
\text{Cov}(X, Y) = \ &[\$1 - \$2.1] \times [\$5 - \$4.6] \times 0.3 \\
&+ [\$2 - \$2.1] \times [\$6 - \$4.6] \times 0.4 \\
&+ [\$3 - \$2.1] \times [\$3 - \$4.6] \times 0.2 \\
&+ [\$4 - \$2.1] \times [\$1 - \$4.6] \times 0.1 \\
= \ &-1.16\$^2
\end{aligned}$$

Note that the covariance is not unit-free. Its unit of measurement is the product of the units of measurement of X and Y, namely $\$ \times \$$, or $\$^2$. The minus sign preceding the covariance value in this example indicates that there is negative association between the market movements of the prices of Stock X and Stock Y. In other words, if X increases, Y decreases and vice versa.

If we now assume that Y is not the price of a single stock but is the market value of a composite stock market index which includes all traded stocks, then the covariance above (-1.16) would indicate that as the stock market (Y) moves up, Stock X moves down and vice versa. Thus, the covariance between X and Y is now a measure of the *systematic (market) risk* or *volatility* of Stock X with respect to market-wide movements.

However, this measure is influenced by the existence of a unit of measurement ($\$^2$), which affects the absolute magnitude of the covariance (1.16) and makes it of limited usefulness. For this reason, we need to convert the covariance into a unit-free index of the *systematic risk* of Stock X. This is precisely how the beta of Stock X is obtained:

$$\begin{aligned}
\text{Beta of } X &= \text{Cov}(X, Y)/\text{Var}(Y) \\
&= -1.16\$^2/2.64\$^2 \\
&= -0.44
\end{aligned}$$

Interpretation

For any risky asset, beta is compared with a benchmark value of 1.00 (which is the beta or volatility of the "market portfolio," e.g., the stock market index used in measuring the beta of Stock X above). Stock X, with a beta of -0.44, is 44% as volatile as the stock market, and moves in the opposite direction to the market. For example, if the value of the stock market index increases by 10%, then there is expected to be a systematic (i.e., market-related, as opposed to asset-specific) change of -4.4% in the market value of Stock X.

Application

Beta, as a measure of *systematic risk*, constitutes one of the key ingredients for determining the appropriate rate of return on any risky asset (security, project, investment, etc.). The conceptual premise underlying the use of beta is that the rate of return we are entitled to expect on a risky asset should not be based on that asset's *total risk*, but only on the *systematic risk* component of the *total risk*. The reason is that the *unsystematic risk* component (see p. 119) of the asset's *total risk* can be diversified away, while the *systematic risk* component cannot. Therefore, our expected return (compensation) for holding a risky asset should be based only on its *systematic risk*, as measured by the asset's beta. This relationship between expected return and beta is the centerpiece of modern capital market theory. In particular, the Capital Asset Pricing Model (CAPM) provides the "Security Market Line" (SML) relationship between the expected return and the *systematic risk* for any risky asset, as follows:

Expected return on asset j = Risk-free rate of interest

$$+ [(\text{Expected market risk premium})$$

$$\times (\text{Beta of asset } j)]$$

or:

$$E(R_j) = R_f + [E(R_m) - R_f] \cdot \beta_j$$

where $E(R_m)$ is the expected return on a stock market index, and R_f is the risk-free rate of interest (e.g., discount rate on a Treasury bill).

Various financial and investment information services provide estimates of betas for widely traded stocks and other securities, as well as for other risky assets. Thus, the user does not always have to carry out the estimation process himself. Also, the long-term average risk premium

$[E(R_m) - R_f]$ on different stock markets is widely available and is fairly stable, so that it can readily be used, along with a given asset's beta, in the process of determining that asset's expected rate of return. For example, suppose the following information is available:

$$R_f = \text{Rate of return on Treasury bill} = 6\%$$

$$E(R_m) - R_f = \text{Expected market risk premium} = 7\%$$

$$\beta_j = \text{Estimated beta for asset or project } j = 1.5$$
(i.e., this asset or project is 1.5 times as volatile as the stock market index).

The expected return on the risky asset or project j can be estimated by using the SML as follows:

$$E(R_j) = 6\% + [(7\%) \times (1.5)] = 16.5\%$$

This estimation allows the investor to make the appropriate decision regarding the asset. If the investor subjectively expects that the return on this asset will actually be higher than 16.5%, then he should buy the asset. If he subjectively expects that the return on the asset will actually be less than 16.5%, then he should not buy the asset, or, if he already holds the asset, he should sell it.

For a risky project, the estimated rate of return (based on the project's estimated beta) can be used to discount the net cash flows forecasted over the project's life, resulting in an estimate of the project's present value. For example, if the beta (1.5) and expected return (16.5%) above pertain to a project which has expected net cash flows of $100, $200, and $50 at the end of years 1, 2, and 3, respectively, and if the project can be undertaken at an initial outlay (price) of $250 today, then the project's net present value (NPV) is:

$$\text{NPV}_j = -\$250 + \$100/(1.165) + \$200/(1.165)^2 + \$50/(1.165)^3$$

$$= -\$250 + \$264.82$$

$$= \$14.82$$

This means that, at a going market price of $250, this project is undervalued by $14.82. Therefore, investing in this project can be expected to add a value of $14.82 to the investing firm's net worth. Of course, if the NPV turns out to be negative, then the project would not be a good investment opportunity and should not be undertaken, since it is an overvalued (overpriced) project.

Systemic Risk (see *Payment System Risk*, p. 80; *Contagion Risk*, p. 11; and *Interbank Risk*, p. 57)

Technological Obsolescence Risk

One of the key factors that must be considered in financing the acquisition of capital equipment or investing in new technology is the risk of technological obsolescence. This is the risk arising from the possibility that a seemingly optimal decision to acquire the services (economic benefits) of a given type of equipment or technology, or to use a specific type of financing for that acquisition, may turn out to be a nonoptimal decision due to rapid advances in technology that may leave the firm locked into using obsolete or inferior equipment.

Technological obsolescence risk may result from uncertainty about or incorrect assessment of the expected useful life of the asset under consideration. Lease financing provides a useful framework for analyzing *technological obsolescence risk*. A firm considering a capital equipment lease may have different options as to the type, duration, payment (annual cost), option to cancel, and other terms of the lease contract. For example, the firm may obtain the use of the equipment under an operating lease contract which requires the firm (lessee) to pay $20,000 at the end of each year for an unspecified term (N years) and is cancelable at the lessee's option at yearly intervals. Alternatively, the firm may take a financial (capital) lease with a fixed annual year-end payment of $16,000 for 8 years without the option to cancel. Note that the lower annual payment under the financial lease is intended to compensate the lessee for the absence of an option to cancel.

All other things equal, the lease contract which costs less in present value (PV) terms will be the more attractive one to the lessee. If the two options have the same PV of cost, that is, if:

$$\frac{\text{PV of \$20,000 per year for } N \text{ years}}{\text{(PV of Operating lease costs)}} = \frac{\text{PV of \$16,000 per year for 8 years}}{\text{(PV of Financial lease costs)}}$$

then the lessee will be indifferent between them. At a discount rate of 4% (the assumed after-tax interest rate that the lessee would have to pay on borrowed funds), this indifference condition can be stated as:

$$\$20{,}000(\text{PVIFA}_{4\%,N}) = \$16{,}000\ (\text{PVIFA}_{4\%,8})$$

where PVIFA stands for the present value interest factor for an annuity at 4% for the number of years indicated. Substituting the value of $\text{PVIFA}_{4\%,8}$ (6.7327, obtained from an annuity table; also available online—see second URL below) and simplifying, the indifference condition becomes:

$$(\text{PVIFA}_{4\%,N}) = (\$16{,}000/\$20{,}000)(6.7327) = 5.3862$$

From the annuity table, it can readily be determined that N is approximately 6.19 years. This means that the lessee would be indifferent between the financial lease and the operating lease if the estimated useful life of the equipment (N) were around 6.19 years. If the lessee chooses the financial lease but N turns out to be less than 6.19 years due to rapid technological obsolescence, then the lessee would incur a loss, as the operating lease and exercising the option to cancel would have been more economical. If the lessee chooses the operating lease but N turns out to be longer than 6.19 years due to technological obsolescence being slow, then the lessee would incur a loss due to continuing to need the equipment, renewing the operating lease each year, and paying higher lease payments ($20,000 instead of $16,000 per year).

The preceding example shows that an accurate assessment of the economic life of capital equipment, including an analysis of competitive and technological factors that might accelerate obsolescence, is instrumental for avoiding or reducing losses from this type of risk.

Term Structure Risk

The term structure of interest rates is the relationship between the yield to maturity (YTM) and the term to maturity, of bonds and other debt instruments that differ only in their term to maturity. The graphical representation of this relationship is called the yield curve and is used widely by financial analysts, economists, bankers, institutional portfolio managers, and others, for analyzing and forecasting movements in market interest rates.

Term structure risk arises from the inability to predict the future course of market interest rates with certainty, given the current level of these rates, and the possibility of making either a gain or a loss as a result of future interest rate movements. A simple example, using one-year and two-year debt instruments, will illustrate the nature of term structure risk.

An Example

Consider an investor who wishes to invest $1,000 for two years in default-free government bonds. Suppose the YTM on a one-year bond is 4%, and the YTM on a two-year bond is 6%. These rates are called the "current spot rates," where the word "spot" indicates that delivery of the bonds is immediate (to distinguish these rates from "future" rates, where delivery of the bonds is at a future point in time). Thus:

k_{0-1} = current (time 0) spot rate on a bond maturing in one year (at time 1)
= 4%
k_{0-2} = current (time 0) spot rate on a bond maturing in two years (at time 2)
= 6%

There are two alternative strategies for this investor over the desired investment horizon of two years, as shown below.

Strategy I: Buy the Two-year Bond

Under this strategy, the investor would carry out the bond investment over the two years in one single step at time 0, and wait until maturity two years from today. At that time, his wealth would be:

$$\$1,000 \times (1 + k_{0-2})^2 = \$1,000 \times (1 + 0.06)^2 = \$1,123.60$$

Strategy II: Buy the One-year Bond and After One Year, Reinvest the Proceeds in Another One-year Bond

Under this alternative strategy, the investor would carry out the two-year investment through two consecutive one-year bonds. However, the investor's wealth at the end of two years would depend on the yield on the second one-year bond k_{1-2}; i.e., his wealth would be:

$$\$1,000 \times (1 + k_{0-1})(1 + k_{1-2}) = \$1,000 \times (1 + 0.04)(1 + k_{1-2})$$

$$= \$1,040 \times (1 + k_{1-2})$$

Term structure risk lies in the fact that the investor's terminal wealth is unknown at time 0, because k_{1-2}, the *future* one-year spot rate, is itself unknown at time 0.

The Forward Rate and the Role of Expectations

The starting point in coping with term structure risk is for investors to estimate the *expected* k_{1-2}. While each investor may arrive at a different subjective expectation of k_{1-2}, there is a unique rate f_{1-2}, implied by the two current spot rates k_{0-1} and k_{0-2}, which may be used in this forecasting process. This rate f_{1-2} is called the one-year *forward* rate and is deduced from the known current spot rates k_{0-1} and k_{0-2} as shown below.

Equate the Wealth Outcomes of Strategies I and II

Since the one-year and two-year bonds in the example are issued by the same issuer (the government) and are free of default risk, there is no risk differential between them that would cause investors to require a higher reward (terminal wealth) from Strategy I or Strategy II. This is to say that at equilibrium, the two strategies would be expected to produce the same wealth outcome at the end of the two-year horizon, that is:

$$\$1,000 \times (1 + k_{0-1})(1 + f_{1-2}) = \$1,123.60$$

or

$$\$1,000 \times (1 + 0.04)(1 + f_{1-2}) = \$1,123.60$$

from which it follows that:

$$(1 + f_{1-2}) = \$1,123.60/[\$1,000 \times (1 + 0.04)] = 1.0804$$

Thus, the one-year forward rate implied by the term structure is $f_{1-2} = 0.0804$ or 8.04%.

Deducing the forward rate in this manner is useful for making a choice between the two strategies above. This can be done by comparing the investor's *subjective* belief about the actual k_{1-2} next year with f_{1-2}. For example, if the investor's subjective expectation is that the actual k_{1-2} next year will be greater than 8.04% (say 8.50%), then he would prefer Strategy II because he would expect it to generate higher terminal wealth than Strategy I:

$$\text{Terminal wealth from Strategy II} = \$1,000 \times (1.04)(1.085)$$

$$= \$1,128.40 > \$1,123.60$$

However, if his subjective expectation is that the actual k_{1-2} next year will be less than 8.04% (say 7.50%), then the investor would prefer Strategy I, since:

$$\text{Terminal wealth from Strategy II} = \$1,000 \times (1.04)(1.075)$$

$$= \$1,118 < \$1,123.60$$

Whether, two years from today, the preferred strategy does turn out to be the more profitable one will of course depend on the realization of the investor's expectations, which is the essence of *term structure risk*.

Total Risk

Total risk is one of the most widely used risk concepts in business, especially in fields such as banking, corporate finance, personal finance, portfolio management, and insurance.

The starting point towards understanding *total risk* is a basic concept of probability: the random variable. A random or probabilistic variable, X, is defined as a variable which could take on a whole range of possible values, with each one of these values having a known (or knowable) probability of occurrence. The probabilities of occurrence of the X values are given by a probability distribution, Prob(X).

The world of business abounds with random variables, and managers have to deal with such variables in virtually every business situation where a decision must be made, and with almost every problem for which a solution must be found. Common examples of random variables from the world of business include future demand and sales, stock prices and rates of return, the level of interest rates, real estate values, and so on.

The concept of *total risk* and its measurement can best be illustrated with an example using a random variable such as the market price of a stock. Suppose an investor believes that the price of a given stock could vary between $1 and $4 ($X$ column below), and that the investor estimates the probabilities shown in the Prob(X) column for the different possible values of X:

X	$Prob(X)$
$1	0.3
$2	0.4
$3	0.2
$4	0.1
	1.0

The probabilities may be based on the investor's subjective beliefs about the stock, or on his analysis of past and present data about the stock, or on any other information available to the investor. Different investors may (and usually do) assign different probabilities to any given value of the stock.

Note that the probabilities can never be negative, and that their sum must always be exactly 1.0 (100%). This rule always holds for any random variable.

To better understand the nature of the above probability distribution of X (stock price), we need to define two characteristics of the distribution: the mean or expected value, and the variance.

The Mean or Expected Value, E(X)

The mean is a measure of central tendency, which is the tendency of all the possible values of X to be centered around or pulled towards some middle value of X. To state this in more familiar words, the mean (middle value) is the investor's expectation about the stock price, or $E(X)$. This expected value is determined as follows:

$$E(X) = (\$1 \times 0.3) + (\$2 \times 0.4) + (\$3 \times 0.2) + (\$4 \times 0.1)$$

$$= \$2.1$$

In essence, this expected value is a weighted average value of the stock price, with the probabilities used as weights.

The Variance, Var(X)

The variance is a measure of dispersion, which is the property of the X values being spread around the mean (i.e., above and below $2.1). For example, the actual stock price could turn out to be $4 (which is higher than the mean or expected value of $2.1), or $1 (which is lower than the mean of $2.1). The greater this total spread of the possible stock prices around the mean stock price ($2.1), the greater the *total risk* of the stock.

The variance measures the *total risk* of the stock price, in the sense that it captures the entire variability of the X values, both upward (above the mean) and downward (below the mean). (See *upside risk*, p. 120, and *downside risk*, p. 21.) In other words, the *total risk* of the stock, as expressed numerically by the variance, is the answer to the investor's question: How far off from the expected stock value could the actual stock values be? This is a different question from: How far *below* the expected stock value could the actual stock values be? The latter question is concerned with the stock's *downside risk* (see p. 21) rather than its *total risk*.

Note that using the variance to answer the former question (i.e., the question about the stock's *total risk*) involves squaring the deviation between each possible value and the expected value, and then adding up these squared deviations after they have been weighted by the respective probabilities. This is illustrated for the stock price data given above:

$$\text{Var}(X) = [(\$1 - \$2.1)^2 \times (0.3)] + [(\$2 - \$2.1)^2 \times (0.4)]$$
$$+ [(\$3 - \$2.1)^2 \times (0.2)] + [(\$4 - \$2.1)^2 \times (0.1)]$$
$$= 0.89$$

The purpose of squaring the deviations from the mean is to avoid losing negative deviations against positive deviations when the addition is carried out. As a result, $\text{Var}(X)$ for this stock is measured in dollars squared; that is, $\text{Var}(X) = \$^2 0.89$. (The standard deviation, discussed below, removes the square from the unit of measurement.)

As a measure of *total risk*, the variance can be used in making risk-return or risk-value comparisons. For example, if there is another stock whose possible market price is denoted by Y, and for which the investor has assigned probabilities and worked out the mean and variance as follows: $E(Y) = \$2.1$ and $\text{Var}(Y) = \$^2 1.25$, then the investor would consider this stock as having greater *total risk* than the previous stock $(1.25 > 0.89)$, for the same expected value of $2.1.

The Standard Deviation, SD(X)

The standard deviation, SD(X), is simply the square root of the variance:

$$SD(X) = \sqrt{Var(X)}$$

In the above illustration, the standard deviation of the stock price is $\sqrt{\$^2 0.89} = \$0.94$. Like the variance, the standard deviation is also a measure of total risk which has two main advantages in application:

■ The unit of measurement is the same as that of the mean. In our stock example, the mean stock price is $E(X) = \$2.1$ and its standard deviation is $SD(X) = \$0.94$. Both are measured in dollars. (By contrast, the stock price variance is measured in dollars squared.)
■ In many applications, especially in portfolio management (see *portfolio risk*, p. 86), the absence of squaring from the standard deviation simplifies the analysis of the risk-return profiles of various alternatives.

As discussed elsewhere, the management of *total risk* involves its decomposition into a *systematic risk* component (see p. 101) and an *unsystematic risk* component (see p. 119).

Trade Noncompletion Risk

In international trade, *noncompletion risk* is an important potential impediment to import–export transactions. *Noncompletion risk* arises from the possibility that, at any stage of an international transaction, one or more of the terms agreed upon between importer and exporter might be construed by either party as not having been fulfilled. This usually leads to halting the remaining stages of the transaction, resulting in losses or additional costs to one or both of the parties to the transaction.

In essence, *noncompletion risk* has its roots in the absence of full trust between importer and exporter. This problem of trust is manifest in the fact that the exporter is usually reluctant to transfer the title to the goods until he receives payment from the importer, while the importer is usually reluctant to pay until title to the goods is transferred to him from the exporter.

A high degree of trust may be established after a long series of identical or similar, trouble-free transactions between two parties, and as a result each party may consider the *noncompletion risk* in future transactions with the other party to be negligible. However, cases like this are not characteristic of the environment of international trade, where *noncompletion risk* (both perceived and actual) in direct dealings between importers and exporters is high, giving rise to substantial demand for protection against this risk.

One factor behind the high level of *noncompletion risk* in international trade is that traders (importers and exporters) do not usually confine their dealings to one counterparty or to few counterparties. A second factor is that long series of identical or similar transactions between the same two parties may be rare or may account for a small proportion of the volume of international trade transactions. A third factor is the uncertainty regarding which country's (or countries') laws are applicable for settling disputes over interpretation or alleged breaches of the terms of an import–export transaction.

Banks play a major role in providing protection against *noncompletion risk*, through the device of the letter of credit. Through this device, banks provide:

- a guarantee (the letter of credit itself) that payment will be made to the exporter if he fulfils his part of the terms and conditions agreed upon with the importer;
- a payment instrument (the draft), through which the exporter actually receives payment; and
- a shipping document (the bill of lading), through which the importer obtains title to and physical delivery of the goods if he fulfils his promise to pay the stipulated price of the goods to the bank.

Transaction Risk

Transaction risk is a type of *exchange rate risk* (see p. 32). It is the possibility of fluctuation in the actual cash flows generated by a project, investment, or subsidiary in a foreign country, as a result of fluctuations in the value of that country's currency. *Transaction risk* must be distinguished from *translation risk* (see p. 118), which arises purely from the accounting treatment of foreign cash flows, and not from actual fluctuations in those cash flows before their translation into the home currency.

An example would be useful in explaining *transaction risk*. Consider the following three entities, *X*, *Y*, and *Z* in three countries, *A*, *B*, and *C*, respectively:

Country:	*A*	*B*	*C*
Entity:	Firm *X*	Project *Y*	Supplier *Z*

Firm *X* owns Project *Y*. The project requires (among other operating expenditures) the use of raw materials provided by Supplier *Z*. The net cash inflow of the project is 1000 units of Currency *B*, before deducting annual cash outflows of 300 units of Currency *B* that must be converted to Currency *C* and paid to Supplier *Z*. Thus, after this payment is deducted, the net cash inflow of the project is 700 units of Currency *B*.

Now assume Currency *B* depreciates by 50% relative to Currency *C*. The result will be that the project's cash outflow going to Supplier *Z* will double (i.e., it will increase from 300 units to 600 units of Currency *B*). This will cause a reduction in the project's net cash flow from 700 units to 400 units of Currency *B*. Even at the same translation rate from Currency *B* to Currency *A*, Firm *X* will see a reduction in its net income from the project. This reduction is due entirely to *transaction risk*.

Among the most widely used techniques for managing *transaction risk*, firms use various strategies involving currency derivatives (futures, options, and swaps). For long-term projects, there may not exist any derivative contracts with long enough maturities to match the term of the project. In such cases, balance sheet hedging strategies may be used (see *translation risk*, p. 118). However, these strategies require careful evaluation of their implications for the firm's cost of capital, as they involve possible changes in the firm's capital structure (debt/equity mix).

Transfer Risk

Transfer risk is one of the two component categories of *country risk* (see p. 11); the other component is *sovereign risk* (see p. 98). *Transfer risk* encompasses a variety of situations in which a non-government foreign borrower faces problems in servicing its debt obligations denominated in hard currencies.

There are several possible factors which, separately or in combination, may give rise to *transfer risk* in some countries. Usually, the main factor is the existence or imminence of a foreign exchange shortage in a given country, often resulting in foreign exchange controls being applied by the government to commercial banks, private-sector firms, and individuals in that country. Another important factor is the adoption, in the foreign country, of international trade policies that use devaluation of the country's local currency as a tool for managing that country's balance of trade.

Examples of situations which give rise to *transfer risk* include the following:

■ A decline in a country's foreign currency reserves, and/or difficulties in generating foreign currency inflows into that country may result in the imposition of foreign exchange restrictions. A private-sector borrower in that country must now request and obtain approval from a designated government agency for every installment payment on its outstanding foreign currency loans. As private-sector borrowers are not usually given high priority by the foreign exchange control agency, approval may be slow or the request may be denied, causing deterioration in the borrower's debt-service ability and increasing the lender's exposure to *transfer risk*.

■ A foreign exchange shortage at the central bank of a given country may prevent the central bank from lending foreign currency to domestic banks, as a "lender of last resort." In turn, the domestic banks and their branches in other countries may face difficulties in honoring requests for withdrawals from foreign currency placements they hold for other banks. As a result, these placements are exposed to greater *transfer risk*.

■ A country that has a growing deficit in its balance of trade may use devaluation of its domestic currency as a policy tool for making exports more attractive and imports more costly. As a result, repayments by domestic firms which have outstanding loans in foreign currencies will become more costly, and their debt service may deteriorate. This possibility is a source of *transfer risk* to the lender.

It should be noted that *transfer risk* differs from *repatriation risk* (see p. 88) in two important respects:

1. *Transfer risk* arises in connection with loans made to private borrowers in another country, and (unlike *repatriation risk*) not in

connection with foreign direct investment (FDI) in that country by multinational firms.

2. *Transfer risk* is entirely the result of foreign exchange shortages and restrictions on hard currency outflows from a given country, and (unlike *repatriation risk*) is not connected to that country's policy regarding its "fair share" of the benefits from FDI.

Translation Risk

Translation risk is a type of *exchange rate risk* (see p. 32). It arises from the accounting treatment of a company's receivables or payables denominated in a fixed amount of some foreign currency.

Between the time of their inception and the time of their settlement, the exchange rate at which these receivables or payables must be translated to the domestic currency may change. As a result, the company may book an accounting profit or an accounting loss, purely as a result of the exchange rate ultimately used as the translation rate.

In the case of foreign-currency receivables, appreciation of the domestic currency at the time of settlement would result in a loss on the domestic-currency equivalent of the foreign-currency receivable. The reason is that the fixed amount of foreign currency would translate to a smaller amount of domestic currency than what was initially recorded as a receivable. In the opposite case, depreciation of the domestic currency would result in a translation profit upon settlement.

In the case of foreign-currency payables, appreciation in the domestic currency would result in a translation profit, while depreciation of the domestic currency would result in a translation loss.

Translation risk must be recognized as a risk that affects only the reported accounting income, and not the actual before-tax cash flow generated from a transaction or project. Nevertheless, it does affect the after-tax income and net cash flow, as taxes paid on the reported accounting income (where the translation profit or loss is captured) are not merely an accounting figure which appears in the income statement, but an actual cash outflow from the firm to the government.

A widely used method for hedging against *translation risk* is balance sheet hedging. This method consists of offsetting receivables denominated in a foreign currency with an equal amount of payables in the same currency, by borrowing that amount for the same maturity as the receivables. Similarly, payables denominated in a foreign currency are offset by lending an equal amount of the same currency for an equal term.

Uninsurable Risks (see *Insurable Risks,* p. 55)

Unique Risk (see *Unsystematic Risk*)

Unsystematic Risk

A prior reading of the discussion of *total risk* (see p. 111) is a prerequisite for understanding this discussion of *unsystematic risk*.

The *total risk* (see p. 111) of an asset, investment, security, or project, consists of two components:

- a nondiversifiable component, known as the *systematic risk* (see p. 101; also known as the *nonspecific risk* or *market risk*); and
- a diversifiable component, known as the *unsystematic risk* (also known as the *specific risk*, *unique risk*, or *nonmarket risk*).

As an example, consider the market price of a given stock. The overall fluctuation in the stock price over time is represented by its *total risk*, and is measured by the variance or standard deviation of the stock price (see p. 111). If one considered carefully the factors that generate this overall fluctuation, it would be possible to classify those factors into two distinct groups:

1. Factors which have a common (but not necessarily equal) effect on all risky assets, investments, securities, and projects, and are not unique or specific to any given asset, security, investment or project. (These factors are discussed under *systematic risk*, p. 101.)

2. Factors which are unique to a particular risky asset, investment, security, or project. Examples of such factors include each firm's unique management style, product characteristics, financial structure, competitive advantages, and so on. Because these factors are unique to each firm and are not derived from variables that affect the entire market or economic system, they are said to give rise to *unsystematic risk* in each risky asset.

To illustrate the concept of firm-specific factors and *unsystematic risk*, consider the common stocks of two automobile manufacturers (e.g., General Motors and Ford). These two companies are active in the same industry and have a great many similarities in production technology, demand conditions, exposure to foreign tariffs, labor resource conditions (e.g., wage demands, strikes), and other common factors. Nevertheless, it is normal that each company has certain distinctive or unique characteristics (management style, financial strengths and weaknesses, etc.) that do not exist in the other company.

Certainly, firms that are selected from widely different industries (e.g., automobile manufacturing and foodstuff packaging) have a greater number of unique factors when compared to one another. Some of these unique factors in one firm may cause its stock value to move upward at a time when the unique factors of another firm in a different industry may cause that firm's stock value to move downward. Thus, forming a portfolio of these stocks would result in diversification of the *unique (unsystematic) risk* of one stock against the *unique risk* of the other. For this reason, the *unsystematic risk* component of an asset's *total risk* is called the *diversifiable risk*.

The essence of portfolio selection and management is to attain the most efficient diversification of the *unsystematic risks* of the assets held in the portfolio (see *portfolio risk*, p. 86).

Upside Risk

Opposite to *downside risk* (see p. 21), *upside risk* is concerned with the optimistic side of investment behavior, through its focus on an investment's potential for overachieving some expected or target rate of return. If this emphasis is excessive and not properly balanced against the investment's *downside risk* potential, then it may result in speculative behavior (see *speculative risk*, p. 99). Such behavior may be inappropriate or legally constrained, as is the case with institutions that are bound by a fiduciary responsibility (see *fiduciary risk*, p. 35), where standards of prudence in investment behavior must be heeded.

The measurement of *upside risk* involves:

- defining all possible outcomes (wealth levels or rates of return) above an expected or target outcome;
- assigning probabilities to these upside outcomes;
- computing a probability-weighted average of the squared deviations of upside outcomes from the expected value, and using this average (called the semi-variance) as a measure of *upside risk*.

To illustrate, consider the possible market prices of two stocks A and B, with their corresponding probabilities:

A	$Prob(A)$	B	$Prob(B)$
$1	0.3	$1	0.1
$2	0.4	$2	0.1
$3	0.2	$3	0.3
$4	0.1	$4	0.5
	1.0		1.0

The means, variances (measures of *total risk*), and semi-variances (measures of *downside risk*) of the prices of these two stocks are shown below.

Means

$$E(A) = (\$1 \times 0.3) + (\$2 \times 0.4) + (\$3 \times 0.2) + (\$4 \times 0.1)$$
$$= \$2.1$$
$$E(B) = (\$1 \times 0.1) + (\$2 \times 0.1) + (\$3 \times 0.3) + (\$4 \times 0.5)$$
$$= \$3.2$$

Variances

$$\text{Var}(A) = [(\$1 - \$2.1)^2 \times (0.3)] + [(\$2 - \$2.1)^2 \times (0.4)]$$
$$\qquad + [(\$3 - \$2.1)^2 \times (0.2)] + [(\$4 - \$2.1)^2 \times (0.1)]$$
$$= 0.89 \, \$^2$$

$$\text{Var}(B) = [(\$1 - \$3.2)^2 \times (0.1)] + [(\$2 - \$3.2)^2 \times (0.1)]$$
$$\qquad + [(\$3 - \$3.2)^2 \times (0.3)] + [(\$4 - \$3.2)^2 \times (0.5)]$$
$$= 0.96 \, \$^2$$

Semi-variances (SV)

$$\text{SV}(A) = [(\$3 - \$2.1)^2 \times (0.2)] + [(\$4 - \$2.1)^2 \times (0.1)]$$
$$= 0.523 \, \$^2$$

$$\text{SV}(B) = [(\$4 - \$3.2)^2 \times (0.5)]$$
$$= 0.320 \, \$^2$$

A comparison of these two stocks' *total risk* and *upside risk* shows that Stock *B* has slightly more *total risk* than Stock *A* (0.96 vs. 0.89), and that it has substantially less *upside risk* (i.e., less upward potential) than Stock *A* (0.320 vs. 0.523).

War, Revolution, Riot, and Civil Commotion Risk

This is a type of *political risk* (see p. 84) which, for a long time, was considered to be an *uninsurable risk* (see p. 119). The reason is that losses arising from exposure to this type of risk were viewed as potentially catastrophic losses, making it necessary to exclude them from the coverage taken under various policies (e.g., life insurance, marine insurance, property, and liability insurance). This exclusion took the form of a war clause or sometimes a WSRCC (war, strike, riot, and civil commotion) clause.

Because of the difficulties in obtaining affordable coverage of *political risk* from private insurers, the World Bank Group set up the Multilateral Investment Guarantee Agency (MIGA) in 1988. The purpose of MIGA is to facilitate foreign direct investment flows into developing countries. For this purpose, MIGA provides investment guarantees to multinational firms against various components of *political risk*, namely *war*, *revolution*, *riot* and *civil commotion risk*, *expropriation risk*, and *transfer risk*.

In recent years, there has been a marked increase in the number of private insurers who underwrite all or some of the components of *political risk*, including *war risks*. However, there has also been a sharp increase in war risk premiums charged for insuring shipping companies, airlines, and other firms operating in countries and regions where armed conflict is impending or already exists. For example, international insurance underwriters imposed steep war risk surcharges on air carriers and shipping lines based in or calling on Sri Lankan air and sea ports, following a rebel attack on that country's international airport on July 24, 2001.

More drastic measures were taken by some US insurers in the aftermath of the September 11, 2001 attacks on the World Trade Center and the Pentagon. Looking at the prospect of having to pay an estimated $70 billion in total claims arising from the attacks, several insurance underwriters canceled their war risk coverage under existing policies. Other insurers still willing to underwrite war risks imposed a $1.25 per-passenger surcharge to be paid by the airlines for coverage (believed by the airlines to be far from adequate) of up to $50 million per incident. To assist airlines in carrying this substantial additional financial burden, the US Government took emergency measures which included the provision of supplemental war risk coverage of another $50 million through the Federal Aviation Administration at a subsidized per-flight premium of $7.50.